DANCING TO HISTORY'S TUNE

History, myth and politics in Ireland

For Katherine Anna

First published 1996
Reprinted (with corrections) 1997
The Institute of Irish Studies
The Queen's University of Belfast,
Belfast

This book has received support from the Cultural Traditions Programme
of the Community Relations Council, which aims to encourage
acceptance and understanding of
cultural diversity.

British Cataloguing-in-Publication Data. A catalogue record for
this book is available from the British Library.

ISBN 0 85389 619 4

Printed by W & G Baird Ltd., Antrim
Cover designed by Rodney Miller Associates

DANCING TO HISTORY'S TUNE

History, myth and politics in Ireland

Brian Walker

The Institute of Irish Studies
The Queen's University of Belfast
1996

ACKNOWLEDGEMENTS

In the research and writing of this book I have been assisted by many individuals. For their willing help and expertise I wish to thank the staff of the library of Queen's University, Belfast, the Belfast Central Library, the Linen Hall Library and the National Library of Ireland. I am grateful to Don Akenson, Jane Leonard, Bill Crawford and Bill Maguire for their comments on early drafts of some of these essays. I greatly appreciated my discussions with Vincent Comerford and George Boyce on the subject of myth and history in Ireland. Bill Vaughan, Jacqueline Hill and Jack Johnston provided important information and valuable ideas.

An earlier draft of chapter one was given as a paper at a conference of the Protestant and Catholic Encounter group at Portadown in November, 1991, and published in the *Irish Review*, no. 12 (Summer, 1992). A version of chapter two appeared in *Nationalism and unionism: conflict in Ireland 1885–1921* (Belfast, 1994), edited by Peter Collins. The *Irish Times*, 3 and 4 January 1993, published a shortened account of chapter six. I have benefited from the comments of colleagues on papers delivered at the annual conferences of the European Society for Irish Studies in Florence, 1994, the American Conference for Irish Studies at Omaha, Nebraska, 1994, and the Irish Australian History Society at Hobart, Tasmania, 1995.

A special word of thanks is due to my colleagues and friends at the Institute of Irish Studies. They have been a constant source of information, ideas and encouragement to me. Catherine Boone and Sarah Gardner gave invaluable help with my manuscript. In his role as copy editor Colm Croker brought to the task his usual skill and knowledge. I would particularly like to thank my wife Evelyn for her unfailing patience and support.

CONTENTS

INTRODUCTION

A belief in the great importance of the past or history in Ireland is widespread. The Downing Street Joint Declaration of December 1993 stated that the most urgent need facing the people of Ireland, north and south, was to remove the causes of conflict, 'to overcome the legacy of history' and to heal the divisions which have resulted. In a speech in September 1995 Sir Patrick Mayhew referred to the 'ancient difficulties of Ireland.' Rev. Ian Paisley has warned many times of the dangers to unionists from their 'traditional enemies.' Mr Dick Spring has declared recently that those actively engaged in the peace process are 'defusing an ancient political time-bomb.'[1] The essays in this book challenge such views of the significance of the past. History is just as important, or as unimportant, in contemporary Ireland as elsewhere. The way that history has been received and understood has changed considerably over time. It is wrong to see our current conflicts as the result of a long, deterministic history or to believe that we have a unique history which ties us in a special way to the remote past. At the same time it is true that ideas of the past, as often contained in various myths, do play a key role in our modern day politics and society. An uncritical acceptance of these myths of the past and a failure to understand how our sense of history has emerged have prevented us from seeing our situation and problems in a realistic light and from appreciating the real impact of our past.

I have had the good fortune to study and to teach both history and politics, particularly as they relate to Ireland. My first interest was modern history which I studied at Magee College, Derry, and Trinity College, Dublin. Under the guidance of the late T.W. Moody I wrote a doctoral thesis on Ulster elections in the 1870s and 1880s. My original degree work contained a section on political science and my first permanent academic job was as a lecturer in political science at The Queen's University of Belfast, where I taught the politics of Northern Ireland and the Republic of Ireland and also comparative politics. The latter subject involved looking at various topics such as nationalism, party systems, and religion and politics, all in a European perspective. At present I lecture in nineteenth century Irish history and twentieth century Irish politics at the Institute of Irish Studies at Queen's University.

This collection of essays, which reflects the above interests, is concerned primarily with the impact of history and myth on the contemporary political life of Ireland, covering both Northern Ireland and the Republic of Ireland. As a historian I am interested in the past, not only in trying to reveal information about our history but also in seeking to understand how our interpretation and memory of the past can be influenced by the present. Very often one's understanding of the past is affected strongly by current needs and interests. Frequently, to suit our own purposes, we create or willingly accept myths of the past. The *Concise Oxford Dictionary* (eighth edition, 1990), defines a myth as a 'widely held but false notion of the past'. Sometimes these myths are based on historical inaccuracies while at other times they arise from selective uses of historical events or developments. At the same time we must take care not to view myths just in a negative light. Often they can be a part of a sense of history, containing truths and half truths, which a group or community can create for itself, in response to contemporary challenges or needs.[2]

As a political scientist, I am also interested in the modern world and in matters which influence this world. The past, especially the myths of the past, can have a direct bearing on the present and can influence how we face and deal with modern problems. While history is no more or no less important in Ireland than elsewhere, people believe that it is. Therefore history, or more often the myths of history, can affect strongly contemporary events. Strictly speaking, history is the study or account of the past, but people sometimes use the terms 'history' and the 'past' interchangeably.

The essays in this book are concerned with various aspects of the subject. They try to give a realistic appreciation of the actual impact of historical events on contemporary affairs, they examine how myths of the past can have a strong influence on present actions, and they look at how our sense of history over subjects like identity can change. They investigate matters in a comparative light, both taking into consideration north/south comparisons and also setting matters in a European context. As elsewhere in the world, we are influenced by what happened in the past, but it is important to differentiate between significant historical events and myths of the past which are either factually incorrect or highly selective. Such myths are often a response to the modern world and to those key historical events and processes which have shaped it. These essays seek to challenge a number of popular misconceptions about the impact of the past and the way history is received and understood.

The first chapter, which deals with the unionist sense of history, shows how events of 1641, 1689 and 1690 came to have special significance for unionists. Because of developments in Ireland in the nineteenth century, especially in its last quarter, these historical events assumed a new, and in many ways mythical, importance. The idea that the protestant community has a collective memory of these events which has been passed from generation to generation from the seventeenth century is questioned. In chapter two we look at the 1885 and 1886 general elections which constituted the key turning-point when unionist/nationalist politics based on a firm protestant/catholic cleavage emerged to set the pattern for late nineteenth and twentieth century politics in Ireland. These recent historical events, not the remote past, have been among the most crucial for the development of our modern world. The religious divisions in Ireland and their impact on politics, which emerge as so influential in this period, are the subject of a special study in chapter three which looks at the matter in its Western European perspective. Perhaps surprisingly for many observers today, it will be seen that religious conflict is a serious political problem found in other European countries over the last hundred years but, perhaps equally surprising to many others, one which has been dealt with more successfully elsewhere than Ireland.

Chapter four looks at how myths of the past impinge on contemporary actions. This chapter is based on a study of references to the past in books, the press and elsewhere over the last five years. It is argued that an over-emphasis on the past as an explanation or excuse for current actions has often been damaging. There is now some evidence of an interesting change in this attitude to history, especially as it affects the conflict in Northern Ireland. Chapter five is concerned with how interest in the past can change, by looking at popular commemorations and observing how they have altered in various ways for different sections of the community. St Patrick's Day, Remembrance Sunday and the twelfth of July are among the commemorations which are examined. Chapter six studies how Irish identity has changed over the last two hundred years and challenges simple assumptions about 'Irishness' and 'the Irish nation'. This emphasises how the understanding of important ideas such as identity or the nation can be affected by historical developments. Finally, chapter seven describes recent published work on the history of Northern Ireland: this serves as evidence of the important ongoing work in the field of Irish historiography.

These essays have been researched and written over the last five years. Some have been published already or delivered at conferences. I have taken advantage of comments from helpful readers or listeners to amend or develop further these papers. Over half of them have not been published before. I hope that, brought together in this collected form, they will help to cast light on the important question of the impact of the past, as expressed in both history and myth on our modern world. The two parts of Ireland are examined in this study, although there is a predominance of material on Northern Ireland reflecting the author's northern base and also his concern with the conflict within Northern Ireland. At the same time a broad Irish context is retained because developments in the north cannot be understood without a knowledge of developments in the south.

In his book *The Irish troubles: a generation of violence 1967–92*, published in 1993, J. Bowyer Bell noted how in other countries people were emboldened to act 'by Lenin's or Mao's example, by Allah's word or the people's need. The enemy was killed by the book.' In Ireland's case, however, Bell states 'he was killed to history's tune.'[3] These essays argue that, many actions in Ireland, north and south, are influenced by 'history's tune.' To put it more correctly, however, it is the myths of our history that influence our actions.

1

1641, 1689, 1690 AND ALL THAT:
THE UNIONIST SENSE OF HISTORY

These three dates mark what are often regarded as key events in unionist and protestant history. 1641 is the date of the outbreak of rebellion and subsequent massacres in Ireland, 1689 is the year of the siege of Derry, and 1690 marks the date of the battle of the Boyne. Any viewing of an Orange parade will reveal frequent reference to these events on the banners. All three are viewed as an essential part of the unionist sense of history. Clearly they have a powerful symbolic value today, but they are also seen as important in affecting the collective protestant consciousness and determining the protestant outlook on the world over a time-span stretching from the seventeenth century to the present day. 1641 represents a time of betrayal and death, 1689 marks a famous siege, while 1690 is the date of a great military victory. These seventeenth century events have remained of major importance to Ulster protestants, it is often asserted, and have given them a strong continuous sense of history.

This view of unionist history is widespread not only among unionists but also among nationalists and outside observers, and is found at both popular and academic level. It is seen as giving unionists in Northern Ireland today a 'siege mentality'. Many unionists themselves regard the conflict in the north as an age-old one and often talk of the 'traditional enemy'.

Others accept this idea of a centuries-old conflict, as we can see, for example, in the comment by Mr John Major on B.B.C. television in February 1992, before a meeting with unionist politicians, that the problems of Northern Ireland are so intractable because they go back to the early seventeenth century. Similarly, in May 1995, after a session of the Forum for Peace and Reconciliation, Mr John Bruton talked on R.T.E. of the legacy of three hundred years of divisions, while Professor Denis Donoghue has stated that 'hostility between catholics and protestants has been an incorrigible feature of life in the North since the Plantation'.[1] This general view is important not just for what it tells us about people's understanding of the past but also because it influences attitudes to the present. The belief that there has been conflict since earliest times and that betrayal and siege are dominating factors of our history clearly affects efforts to change the current impasse.

Serious questions must be raised, however, about this whole approach. Is there, in fact, any real evidence of a protestant sense of history, a folk memory, which has been passed from generation to generation from the seventeenth century to the present and which marks these events out as vitally significant? Have these events *always* been important? Clearly many people regard them as relevant today, but is there a real sense of continuity from the seventeenth century to the present? How have unionists arrived at their idea of history? How does the present influence our understanding of the past? How does our understanding of the past influence current actions?

These three events are worth further examination. 'As a watershed in protestant history', Dr Bill Rolston has remarked, in his study of political wall murals in Northern Ireland 'the significance of the year 1690 is stamped indelibly on the protestant collective consciousness in Ireland'.[2] Yet, in the late eighteenth century, a mere one hundred years after the Boyne, there is no evidence that it was regarded as a great event by the protestants of Ulster. The *Belfast Newsletter* for July 1790 carries no account of any centenary celebrations in Belfast. It does report, however, commemorations in

Downpatrick (Co. Down) and Doagh (Co. Antrim). In these two centres the Boyne was celebrated not as a great protestant triumph but as a constitutional victory. A toast to the memory of King William was followed by toasts to the Irish Volunteers and the American revolution. According to the *Belfast Newsletter*, the anniversary of William's birthday on 4th November 1790 was marked in Belfast only by a dinner of the Northern Whig Club, where twenty-five toasts were drunk to various Whig and reformist causes.[3]

As regards the siege of Derry, the social anthropologist Dr Anthony Buckley has commented: 'Of all these historical events, this siege has the greatest symbolic significance'.[4] But if we look at how the event was commemorated one hundred years afterwards, it is clear that it has not always had this importance. In 1789 processions and events were staged in Derry to celebrate the centenary of the siege, but they were far from being exclusive protestant celebrations.[5] In August 1789, to mark the centenary of the relief of the city, a large procession took place to the Church of Ireland cathedral and included the catholic bishop, Philip McDevitt, and several of his clergy. Rather than being seen simply as a protestant victory, the siege was celebrated as a triumph of liberty.

What of the 1641 uprising and massacres? It is not at all clear how far this event was remembered as a genuine folk memory. Writing in the 1880s, the presbyterian farmer and local historian W. F. McKinney described atrocities in his own area of east Antrim in the 1640s.[6] However, he set this in the context of greatly exaggerated figures of protestant deaths which were being commonly bandied around in the second half of the nineteenth century, and it is unlikely that anything of all this reflected a deep-seated historic memory. Indeed, McKinney, who was an expert family historian, reckoned that there were very few families in his area which went back to the early seventeenth century. Most had arrived later than 1690: many earlier families had moved on. So in this area at least it seems unlikely that there was a real folk memory of what happened in the 1640's.

But for McKinney, and for many other Ulster protestants, events of 1641, along with those of 1689 and 1690, became

very significant in the course of the nineteenth century. Two
hundred years after the original dates we find extensive commemorations: by this stage they were regarded clearly as an
important part of the sense of history shared by many protestants. Increased emphasis on these dates was occasioned in
the later nineteenth century, partly because in the 1870s the
English historian J.A. Froude drew considerable attention to
the 1641 massacres and Lord Macaulay described the siege
of Derry in a famous piece of narrative prose in the 1860s.[7]
Much more importantly, because of the new circumstances of
the nineteenth century, which arose with the deepening of
religious division and rise of unionism and nationalism, especially in the 1880s, these seventeenth-century dates became
significant and relevant to people seeking to justify their contemporary positions. These events fitted well into the new
historical perspective that protestants were making for
themselves, in response to the changing conditions of their
modern world.

Protestants would soon forget the 1798 rebellion, in which
many presbyterians participated as United Irishmen, and
remember instead certain seventeenth-century events.
Indeed, probably more east Antrim protestants were killed by
crown forces at the battle of Antrim in 1798 than by rebels in
1641, yet in the 1880s these later deaths were forgotten and
the earlier ones recalled. The events of 1641, 1689 and 1690
were undoubtedly important for seventeenth century
Ireland, but when they are remembered today it is because
they were recalled again in the nineteenth century (after they
had largely faded from memory) and have remained an
important part of the modern protestant consciousness. The
genuine depth of this new sense of history and its contemporary implications can be seen clearly in people such as
McKinney, who lost a great-uncle at the battle of Antrim in
the ranks of the United Irishmen, but later sacrificed a grand-
son at the battle of the Somme in the British army.

Obviously it would be foolish to claim that these events
were totally forgotten in the eighteenth century and the first
half of the nineteenth century. The 1641 rising remained a
subject for special sermons in the Church of Ireland in the

eighteenth century, although the printing of such sermons
had apparently ceased by the 1770s and the official commemoration of 23 October (the day of the rebellion's outbreak) by the viceroy ended in the 1780s.[8] King William's
birthday on 4 November was an officially recognised anniversary until 1806, although reformers in Ireland saw him as a
hero of theirs until the late 1790s when he became an Orange
hero.[9] Clearly the siege of 1689 in Derry was not forgotten in
the city, but the Apprentice Boys of Derry, who boosted the
event as a great protestant victory, were not established until
the early nineteenth century.[10] The Orange Order, which did
assign great importance to these events, was founded only in
1795. Canon S.E. Long, the Orange historian, has remarked
on how the new Orange movement adopted its historical
basis:

> It is not to undervalue the Williamite connection to argue that it
> was a convenient historical peg on which to hang a movement
> with goals which bore more than a passing similarity to those of
> King William III. Having made the point it could be argued
> further that the 17th century historical ancestry of Orangeism
> was an accretion valuable for its imagery, symbolism, similarity
> and success but not something intrinsic to Orangeism which
> came out of historical crises of another age with motivations and
> attitudes of its own.[11]

While not forgotten, these events were not major ones to
be commemorated every year by the bulk of the protestant
population. Indeed, while they became more important for
more people in the nineteenth century, this was a gradual
process. Until the last decades of the nineteenth century
there were still large sections of the protestant population for
whom they were not viewed as matters of great interest
or relevance. After the emergence of nationalist/unionist
confrontation in the 1880s, however, interest in these
historic events became significantly more widespread than
before. In 1922 Ronald McNeill, later Lord Cushendun,
commented about the impact of the home rule issue in
1885/6:

The 'loyalist' tradition acquired fresh meaning and strength, and its historical setting took a more conscious hold on the public mind of Ulster, as men studied afresh the story of the relief of Derry or the horrors of 1641.[12]

The Orange Order, with its emphasis on this historical setting, had been a minority movement among protestants until well after the mid-1880s. The bulk of presbyterians, in particular, remained outside its ranks until later. McNeill observed how in the years before 1886 the Order had fallen into 'not unmerited disrepute,' but after the introduction of Gladstone's home rule bill it received an 'immediate accession of strength':

> Large numbers of country gentlemen, clergymen of all protestant denominations, business and professional men, farmers, and the better class of artisans in Belfast and other towns, joined the local lodges, the management of which passed into capable hands; the character of the Society was thereby completely and rapidly transformed, and, instead of being a somewhat disreputable and obsolete survival, it became a highly respectable as well as an exceedingly powerful political organisation, the whole weight of whose influence has been on the side of the Union.[12]

Historians, such as J.C. Beckett, and local case studies, have emphasised how significant this post 1885–6 period was for both the numerical strength and importance of the Orange Order with its historical traditions.[13]

The growing interest in the seventeenth century is well illustrated in examples of Williamite engraved glass. Until recently this engraved glass was seen as evidence of continuing eighteenth century interest in William, but now, thanks to the work of Peter Francis, we know that this glass was engraved by a late Victorian Dublin artist who catered for the new and expanding interest in William at the end of the nineteenth century.[14] The Williamite glass was a complete artifice of the late nineteenth century which has seemed evidence of a longstanding tradition. Various Orange traditions did have a genuine lineage, going back to the late eighteenth century.

In the last decades of the nineteenth century, however, the expression of these traditions changed in a number of ways (see chapter 5), and, more importantly, they now became meaningful and relevant for a much wider section of the protestant community. Social historian Eric Hobsbawm has shown how the creation or 'invention' of tradition was a common feature of many social groups at this time in Europe and North America, in response to profound changes in the political and social order of the late nineteenth and early twentieth centuries.[15]

Changes in attitude to the past are reflected clearly in the writings of Thomas Witherow, Thomas MacKnight and Lord Ernest Hamilton. Thomas Witherow (1824–90) was a presbyterian minister, first professor of church history in Magee College, Derry, and a liberal. His book *Derry and Enniskillen in the year 1689: the story of some famous battlefields in Ulster* was published in Belfast in 1873 and rapidly ran into several reprints. In his introduction he explained that he wrote from 'an entirely protestant standpoint' but that he had endeavoured 'to look at the matter with the eye of a historian, and to deal out even-handed justice to all'. He pointed out that courage and gallantry were not all on one side. He then stated:

> It is no time now to revive the bitter feuds and enmities of the past; and should the writer, in expressing his opinion freely in regard to men and things, have unconsciously said a word to excite a feeling of bitterness in any man towards his neighbour, it would be to him an unfailing source of regret. Such a feeling is not in his own heart.

He advised people not to be embroiled in the controversies of the past.

> He would much rather teach his countrymen, if he could, to look at the past in a calm and kindly spirit, to rise superior to the passions of an evil age, and henceforth to rival each other, not in fields of blood and war, but in the arts of industry and peace.[16]

This approach can be contrasted usefully with the opening chapter of the first volume of Thomas MacKnight's two-volumed *Ulster as it is* (London, 1896), which recounted his experience as editor of the liberal Belfast paper, the *Northern Whig*, from 1866 to 1894. The book described efforts to push the liberal cause in Ulster, but was written after the crucial general elections of 1885–6 when the liberal attempts to create a non-denominational party finally collapsed in front of the newly emerging unionist and nationalist parties based solidly on religious division. At the end of his career he chose to begin his memoirs by recalling a conversation in 1866 with a clergyman in Portadown on his first visit to Ulster.[17] The clergyman informed him of protestant deaths in Portadown in 1641 and warned him of the long memories of people in Ulster. Clearly MacKnight recalled this later and decided to start his book with the story because, after all his efforts to further non-sectarian politics, it seemed in retrospect a good reason for his failure. In light of the new order of politics and religion to emerge so firmly in 1885–6 this historical perspective now offered a reasonable explanation for the outcome.

Finally, we may consider the writings of Lord Ernest Hamilton, unionist M.P. for North Tyrone, 1885–92, and the author of a number of historical works. His volume *The soul of Ulster* published in 1917 spelt out clearly the lessons of the past as he saw them. He believed that religious differences had little to do with the situation and argued that the Ulster protestant had been involved continually in a stark conflict over land and between 'races' from the time of the 1641 bloodshed which 'laid the seeds of an undying distrust'. He stated:

The fundamental idea at the back of the Ulsterman's attitude is that what has once happened may well happen again. It is argued that when, throughout a period of several hundred years, certain occurrences have invariably succeeded the opportunity for such occurrences, it is not unreasonable to assume that – given the same opportunities – the same occurrences will again make appearance.

He urged English politicians to read the historical facts, so
that 'they might ultimately arrive at the great truth that the
soul of the native Irish has not at the present day changed by
the width of a hair from what it was in 1641, and again in
1798'.[18]

The new unionist sense of history, which emerged clearly
in its modern form in the late nineteenth century, ignored
several important aspects of protestant history. First, it
glossed over the fact that for much of that history, presbyterians and members of the Church of Ireland have been
strongly at odds.[19] Sections of the eighteenth century penal
laws affected presbyterians. Although Rev. Henry Cooke the
influential presbyterian leader had in the 1830s urged an
alliance of the two denominations, considerable hostility
remained between them. In part this hostility arose from religious differences, but also it was caused by resentment among
presbyterians against the high social and political position of
some Church of Ireland members. Even in 1880 the presbyterian *Witness* complained about Church of Ireland influence
in government circles: 'From the very highest official to the
lowest, there is a disposition to keep episcopacy in a position
of ascendancy'.[20] This questions the idea of a longstanding
united protestant struggle.

Secondly, this view of history forgot the times when there
was either peaceful coexistence or co-operation between
protestant and catholic, and when the great events of the seventeenth century were not in people's minds. There are
many instances in the nineteenth century, especially in the
first three-quarters of that century, of protestant contribu-
tions for new catholic churches.[21] J. A. Rentoul, a presbyterian minister and a unionist M.P., in his autobiography *Stray
thoughts and memories*, published in 1921, recorded the good
relations between clergy of the different denominations in
Donegal in the period from the 1850s to the 1880s.[22] He
described how Daniel McGettigan, when catholic bishop of
Raphoe in the 1850s, had regarded his father, a presbyterian
minister, as 'a co-worker engaged with him in a common war,
though fighting under different regimental colours'.
Political alliance occurred between sections of catholics and

presbyterians, not only in 1798 but also in the movement for
land reform in the period 1850-80.[23] All this contradicts the
simplistic view of confrontation and unending struggle going
back to the early seventeenth century.

The unionist sense of history, therefore, with its great
emphasis on 1641, 1689 and 1690, and with the accompanying idea of constant conflict between protestant and catholic,
is highly selective. The marked lack of interest in these events
during the eighteenth century and much of the nineteenth,
along with information about sharp protestant division at
some times and presbyterian-catholic alliance at other times,
is conveniently forgotten in this historical account. However,
while this recall of history was incomplete and in many ways
artificial, it did and does relate to a very real situation. In
Ireland in the late nineteenth century and in Northern
Ireland today there was and is a genuine conflict over religion
and nationalism. People have used and do use historical arguments to strengthen their resolve and to explain to themselves and to others why all this has happened.

The reality of this conflict, which first appeared in its modern form in the 1880s, must be appreciated fully. The sharp
divisions in politics, with protestant and unionist on the one
hand, and catholic and nationalist on the other, emerged in
Ulster at the general elections of 1885–6 and have remained
ever since at the nub of our situation, in spite of constitutional and territorial changes. In chapter two we look at how
religion and nationalism became intertwined firmly in this
crucial period, giving us the particular type of politics and
sectarian confrontation found today. This outcome was not
an inevitable one, in spite of past religious and political conflicts. Developments in late nineteenth-century Ireland, especially the deepening of religious divisions, along with the
electoral manoeuvring and political decisions by party leaders, crucially helped to shape the particular form of sectarian
divisions that emerged at this time and set the scene for present day Northern Ireland .

For many unionists, then, such as Thomas MacKnight and
Lord Ernest Hamilton, and for many people today, the new
unionist and protestant history, with its emphasis on the great

seventeenth century events and their continued relevance, seemed and still seems a good explanation for why these conflicts emerged as they did. However, not only is this sense of history selective and incomplete, but it ignores the fact that the modern problems of division over religion and nationalism in Ulster are common ones found in countries in Western Europe, a point missed by many, in both the nineteenth and twentieth centuries. The situation in Ulster in the 1880s, and in Northern Ireland at the present time, was and is not based on a unique history. With very different histories, other countries in Western Europe at the end of the nineteenth century also encountered similar political divisions over these matters. While of a type not generally found in the mainstream Anglo-American political world – and for that reason requiring special historical explanation – the situation in Ulster in the 1880s and in Northern Ireland at the present time was and is by no means unique.

When we look at Western Europe at the end of the nineteenth century, we discover that in various countries (such as Germany, Holland and Switzerland) with protestant-catholic cleavages, and others (such as Italy and Belgium) with clerical and anticlerical cleavages, politics were also divided sharply by religion.[24] Nationalism was a source of political division in countries as varied as Italy and Norway.[25] The situation in Ulster was unusual only in the particular intertwining of religion and nationalism, but this related to specific developments in Ireland in the 1880s and was not due to any unique history. These problems elsewhere in Western Europe did not disappear with the twentieth century, a fact that we often forget. Religion, in particular, has remained a key dividing factor between parties in many countries, whether between protestants and catholics or between church-going and non-church-going catholics.

At the same time, we should note that these countries have found ways of accommodating such differences. In Holland, for example, religious division remained a key factor in political allegiance in the country right up to the mid-1970s, but the Dutch evolved a political system which allowed these differences to coexist peacefully and effectively.[26] The Christian

Democrats, with their religious origins, are the second largest party in the European parliament today, but this does not create a special problem. In both Italy and Norway nationalist divisions within each country have diminished because the successful nationalist movements in the long term dealt with their opponents' objections and integrated or assimilated them into the new nations. So problems over religious division and nationalism can be coped with. At the same time, the frequent occurrence of conflict arising from these causes in Eastern Europe today shows how these problems remain in other parts of Europe as very real contemporary difficulties.

The evidence, therefore, about the events of 1641, 1689 and 1690, and when they became important to Ulster protestants, must lead one to question seriously the idea of a continuous sense of unionist history, based around these events of the seventeenth century, coming uninterrupted from that time to the present. People later came to believe this and still do today: but for many protestants, as for many catholics, their sense of history has been conditioned strongly by the modern needs of the late nineteenth and twentieth centuries. This view of history, with its accompanying idea of constant conflict between protestant and catholic must also be criticised because it fails to take into account other important aspects of protestant history, such as times of protestant disunity and catholic/protestant co-operation. It is a selective record which originally became widespread only in the late nineteenth century. It served to unite protestants in a purposeful sense that was understandable to them and the wider world, in response to the new political confrontation which developed at this time.

The problems of religious division and nationalist/unionist conflict which emerged in the last decades of the nineteenth century in Ulster were not unique ones relating to a special history, going back to 1600 or indeed to 1200. Many other countries, with very different backgrounds, also faced these problems. The remote past may have influenced to a small extent what developed in the 1880s, but, given the experience in other parts of Western Europe where there were religious differences, there was little likelihood that

Ulster would avoid the emergence of religion as a key factor in the community's present-day politics. Nationalism was a common phenomenon in many parts of Europe, in spite of different historical experiences. The political situation in Northern Ireland is no more rooted in our distant history than politics elsewhere, even if people have felt it necessary to explain the situation largely in such historical terms. As Estyn Evans acutely observed in 1951:

> 'Remember 1690' – another of those crisp Ulster wall-slogans - is not the motto of an historical cult (which insists on remembering the Battle of the Boyne where protestant William of Orange defeated the catholic King James on 1st July 1690) so much as the reminder of present day threats to the Ulsterman's security and independence.[27]

Unionist historical beliefs and the criticism that can be made of them have an important bearing on current attitudes. If one believes that the struggle between the two major groups in Northern Ireland has been continuous since early times, then it is difficult to see a resolution to our problems: either they will continue for ever, or there will be a complete victory of one side or the other. Such a view leaves little room for compromise and obviously helps to create a 'siege mentality' with all its implications for current politics. The evidence, however, that this sense of history is inadequate because it fails to take into account quiet times, when the great events of the seventeenth century were largely forgotten and when there was peaceful coexistence or co-operation between the communities, suggests that confrontation is not the only option. This shows that our problems today are not inevitable because of our history. Again, when we appreciate the European perspective on the situation, we realise that these difficulties are not unique to us and unavoidable because of some special historical roots. Divisions over religion and nationalism are common modern European problems which many other countries have faced and have managed to cope with much better than we have. This means that our current conflicts are not inevitable nor insoluble due to our remote past.

Nationalists also developed an important historical sense.[28] In response to the political and religious confrontation of the nineteenth century and early twentieth centuries a strong nationalist view of history emerged. It linked modern nationalism to the idea of a seven centuries-old, continuous struggle of the Irish people with England. It would emphasise certain historical episodes and create its own heroes and villains. Many aspects of the nationalist historical view had emerged by the middle of the nineteenth century (thanks, in large part, to the Young Irelanders), but in the latter decades of the century they took on new forms and became widespread among, and relevant to, more people than previously. As with the unionist view of history, the nationalist view was very selective. It ignored the times when nationalist issues were not to the fore, when Irish people were divided over their future, and when they were not all committed to the idea of an Irish republic. In addition, it treated Ireland's position as unique and linked to a special history.

It is important to understand how our sense of history has been shaped. For unionists, as for nationalists, history has often meant a view of the past influenced very much by the needs of our late nineteenth–and twentieth–century world. It is vital to realise what this sense of history tells us, and also what it omits. We need to see a fuller historical picture which views things in a broader European perspective. Historical knowledge can help illuminate our situation today, but it is essential that we do not allow a selective and inaccurate understanding of the past to set the agenda and compound our problems.

2

THE 1885 AND 1886 GENERAL ELECTIONS – A MILESTONE IN IRISH HISTORY

In the recent history of Ireland, both north and south, certain events are seen in retrospect to have been crucial in establishing the basis of our parties and political divisions. Modern politics in the republic are viewed as rooted in the 1916 rising in Dublin and in the civil war of the early 1920s, while politics in Northern Ireland are regarded as based on the outcome of the events of 1912–14 and the government of Ireland act of 1920. Undoubtedly these episodes were very important, but it should be realised that they influenced a political situation that had already emerged in its essential form at the general elections of 1885 and 1886.[1] These elections saw the birth of modern political parties based on a new mass electorate that embraced nearly every household in the country. Even more significantly, these years witnessed the emergence, for the first time throughout Ireland, of distinct nationalist/unionist politics linked to a clear protestant/catholic division. Later events of 1912–23 would determine the final shape of the territorial and constitutional structures for the two new political units of modern Ireland, but the outcome of these two crucial elections established the basic character of late-nineteenth and early twentieth-century politics in both parts of the country.

Conflict over nationalism was not new to elections in 1885-6, but in the past there had usually been a wide range of political opinion and swings in popular support often occurred. Daniel O'Connell's repeal party and the Young Irelanders had laid the grounds for a nationalist movement. In the 1850s and 1860s, however, the political scene in Ireland had been dominated by the liberal and conservative parties which accepted the United Kingdom framework. It was not until the general election of 1874 with the appearance of the home rule movement, linked to the issues of land and educational reform, that constitutional nationalism became again an important political force. Even so, the general election of 1880 returned not only 62 home rule M.P.s, but also 15 liberals and 26 conservatives. There were important regional variations. On the eve of the 1885 general election, 3 home rulers only, plus 9 liberals and 17 conservatives represented the nine counties of Ulster compared with 62 home rulers, 7 liberals and 9 conservatives for the rest of Ireland.[2]

Rivalry between denominations was also not new to Irish politics in 1885, but at previous elections the influence of religious division in relation to political matters was rarely clear-cut. While protestants tended to vote conservative and catholics were likely to vote liberal, there were times of noticeable exception such as the general election of 1859 when many catholics voted conservative, and the general elections of 1868-80 when many protestants, in particular northern presbyterians, backed the liberal cause. The home rule party won largely catholic support, although in 1874 and 1880 there were considerable numbers of protestant home rule MPs. Elections before 1885 reflected reasonably well changes in political attitudes, although the franchise was restricted to limited categories of property owners and occupiers. There were some well-run local political associations in Ireland before 1885, especially in Ulster, but party organisation in the constituencies was for the most part conducted on an *ad hoc* basis.

From 1885-6 onwards, however, conflict over the nationalist issue, based very largely on a protestant/catholic divide, remained at the centre of Irish elections right up to 1921 and significantly affected the nature of politics that emerged after 1921 in Northern Ireland and the Irish Free State. These political divisions were strongly felt throughout the whole community, owing to the new household vote and effective political organisations, both local and central. The first part of this study will look at the social, economic and religious background. The second part will be concerned with an account of the elections followed by an analysis of the polling. Finally the impact of political developments in these two years must be examined and an explanation given as to why the outcome of these two general elections has proved to have had such a lasting significance.

I

To understand the significance of the elections of 1885 and 1886 it is essential that the political events surrounding them should not be viewed in isolation. Social and economic factors formed an important background to the rise of nationalism and unionism in Ireland. In 1841 the population of Ireland was three times that of Scotland and more than half that of England and Wales.[3] Fifty years later, however, after the Famine and continuous emigration in Ireland and massive industrialisation in Great Britain, the picture was very different. By 1891, Ireland's population had fallen to slightly less than that of Scotland and one eighth of the population of England and Wales.[4] Such developments helped to encourage nationalism. To many nationalists this population decline was seen as linked to the union. In November 1885 Parnell's lieutenant Thomas Sexton declared: 'We look back to the year of the union, along that level plain of years to see the shameful, the miserable results of English rule in Ireland... The population of Ireland was greater than now, the comfort of the people was greater'.[5]

In Ulster the nineteenth-century social and economic experience was rather different. Although parts of Ulster witnessed population decline similar to that elsewhere in Ireland, other parts, especially in the north-east, experienced considerable prosperity, as a result of industrialisation. In 1841 Ulster's population was 29 per cent of that of the whole

of Ireland, but by 1891 it stood at 34 per cent. In 1841
Belfast's population was 70,447, or one-third of Dublin's population of 232,726, but by 1891 Belfast's figure was 276,114
compared with Dublin's 269,716.[6] Belfast grew faster than any
other urban centre in the British Isles in the second half of
the nineteenth century. The Grand Trades Arch in Donegall
Place in Belfast for the royal visit of 1885 captured well the
spirit of Victorian Belfast with slogans such as 'Trade is the
golden girdle of the globe' and 'Employment is nature's
physician'.[7] For unionists in Ulster the period of the union
was seen as a time of rising prosperity.

The land question was another source of division between
Ireland and Great Britain and between Ulster and the rest of
Ireland. The Great Famine, with its enormous human toll,
affected Ulster far less than elsewhere in Ireland, thanks to
northern industrialisation and the availability of crops other
than the potato. After the Famine, rising agricultural prices
brought a growth in prosperity throughout the Irish countryside,[8] but the question of tenure continued as a major source
of discontent until the reforms of the 1880s which followed
the land war of 1879–81. In Ulster, however, farmers benefited from the 'Ulster custom' which gave certain rights to
farmers. While this custom had weaknesses, which were to
help cause tenant unrest at various points in the nineteenth
century, it gave greater security to Ulster farmers than elsewhere and, as a result, the question of land reform, whether
in the early 1850s or the 1870s, seems to have caused less bitterness in the north than elsewhere.

Such major social and economic divisions, which influenced the rise of Irish nationalism, could have helped to create a straightforward split between a totally unionist Ulster
and the rest of Ireland which was entirely nationalist. To
understand why this did not happen it is essential to look at
the religious factor. In 1881 catholics formed about 76 per
cent of the Irish population, while in Great Britain the population was predominantly protestant. Within Ireland protestants were 24 per cent of the total population, and only 9 per
cent outside Ulster, but they were in a small majority in the
whole province of Ulster and a substantial majority in the

north-east. Three-quarters of Irish protestants were to be found in Ulster, but catholics in Ulster were only one-fifth of their whole community in Ireland.[9] For catholics and protestants in nineteenth-century Ireland both religious conflict and the strength of denominational bonds had an important impact on their political positions. Religious division was important not only between Ireland and Britain but within Irish society.

Religious issues such as catholic emancipation had been the cause of considerable political unrest in the first half of the nineteenth century. Although most specifically religious issues were settled by the 1870s, this denominational factor still coloured people's views on broader political matters, including the question of the link with Great Britain and community relations within Ireland. Religious controversies, particularly that over education, continued to cause catholic disillusionment with Westminster, a feeling not experienced by protestants. The strengthening of denominational ties and identities in Ireland, influenced greatly by the revivalism which occurred among all the main denominations in the second half of the nineteenth century, meant that for most people in Ireland, the links with their respective religious groups were very important.[10] Until the mid 1880s, nonetheless, the correlation between religious and political divisions was far from complete. There were sharp divisions in voting behaviour between presbyterians and members of the Church of Ireland in Ulster and there were differences between catholics in Ulster and elsewhere in how they voted.

During 1885–6, however, denominational ties and identities emerged as the main determining factor in political behaviour, regardless of regional or class differences. In these years nearly all Ulster catholics, of every social rank, identified with the political aspirations of their co-religionists elsewhere in Ireland and voted nationalist. In March 1886, Patrick MacAllister, the new catholic bishop of Down and Connor, expressed his satisfaction at 'seeing the catholics of Belfast working in harmony with those of the rest of Ireland in the cause of nationality'.[11] Most protestants, presbyterians

as well as members of the Church of Ireland, in Ulster and in
the rest of Ireland, came together in support of the union,
although only in Ulster were they able to elect unionist MPs.
Social and economic differences between Ulster and the rest
of Ireland go part of the way to help explain the rise of
nationalism and unionism, but in the new political align-
ments that finally emerged in 1885-6, the division between
protestant and catholic proved of great importance.

Economic and social tensions between protestant and
catholic probably played some part in the rise of the opposing camps of unionist and nationalist, but their importance
should not be exaggerated, chiefly because the other main
divisions and conflicts in society did not correlate to a simple
protestant/catholic divide. Members of the Church of
Ireland owned most of the land and dominated official
positions, at the expense not just of catholics but also of
presbyterians. In many parts of Ulster, catholics were over-
represented among unskilled labourers and small farmers
while presbyterians dominated the skilled jobs and the larger
farm sector, but many ordinary members of the Church of
Ireland had little or no special advantage in these latter
areas.[12] Social divisions in Ireland often crossed religious divisions. In the long run, however, religion served not only to
provide a key source of grievance, namely education, but it
united people on a denominational community basis. The
new political arrangements of 1885-6 now established firmly
the link between parties and religious division.

II

In addition to the underlying social, economic and religious
factors affecting Irish life in the 1880s, changes in electoral
law provided important new conditions for the crucial general elections of 1885 and 1886. As a result of the 1883 cor-
rupt practices act, the amount of money that candidates
could spend on their election campaigns was restricted, and
so new, voluntary party organisations were now required.
Throughout the country, constituencies of roughly equal size
were established by the 1885 redistribution act, which also

expanded the number of constituencies from 64 to 101. The franchise act of 1884 extended the vote to adult male house-holders and thus increased the number of Irish voters by over 200 per cent between 1884 and 1885; important sections of the population, in particular the labourers and small farmers, were now enfranchised for the first time.[13] A parliamentary return of 1884-5 showed catholic majorities in all constituencies except for half of the Ulster divisions. These changes presented the existing parties with considerable problems and opportunities.

Other challenges also faced the parties on the eve of the 1885 general election. Throughout the community there was a heightened sense of political consciousness, aroused originally over the land question. Agrarian protest had not only resulted in the 1881 land act, which gave farmers new rights, but it had also undermined the landlords, who had traditionally played a key role in Irish politics. After the 1881 Tyrone by-election one observer commented: 'The fact is the protestants as well as the Roman catholics do not want an Orangeman or even a Fenian if he is a gentleman or a land-lord'.[14] By 1885 landlord-tenant relations were no longer the major issue, which meant that other divisions such as between farmers and labourers, urban and rural interests, and protestant and catholic, assumed new importance for the parties, as did interest groups and internal conflicts.

The various parties responded in different ways to these new challenges. After the 1880 general election C. S. Parnell had taken over the leadership of the home rule party, the largest party in Ireland with 63 seats, but until 1885 it remained a loosely organised body with little discipline among the members in parliament and *ad hoc* organisational structures in the constituencies. In early 1885 it was reckoned that Parnell could count on the wholehearted support of only some 20-30 MPs of his home rule group, and he also had to deal with both agrarian activists and radical nationalist elements.[15] Parnell, however, was also head of the National League, which had been set up to harness agrarian and nationalist protest after the suppression of the Land League. During 1885 the home rule movement underwent marked reorganisation and growth under the direction of Parnell and his followers in the National League.

In common parlance the term 'homeruler' gave way to 'nationalist'. The National League provided for the nationalist party an effective organisation through its local branches which expanded rapidly in 1885. County conventions selected parliamentary candidates, under the supervision of representatives from the organising committee of the league, which was controlled by Parnell. A pledge was introduced to bind the MPs together into a tightly disciplined party. Thus, as Dr Conor Cruise O'Brien has remarked, the National League turned the home rule movement from a loose grouping of independent elements into a 'well-knit political party of a modern type ... effectively monopolising the political expression of national sentiment'.[16] This reorganisation allowed the nationalist party to face the general election very effectively. The National League embraced small farmers and labourers as well as larger farmers and so helped to mitigate chances of social division. Efforts by Michael Davitt and others to radicalise the movement, in particular to organise the labourers, were thwarted and the influence of nationalist radicals was largely destroyed.

Vital for this socially cohesive, countrywide organisation was the forging of a 'very effective, if informal, clerical-nationalist alliance', as Professor Emmet Larkin has called it.[17] Acceptance of catholic claims on education won the party the approval of the hierarchy in mid-1885. The intervention of Archbishop William Walsh of Dublin ensured that all catholic clergy should have the right to attend nationalist conventions to select parliamentary candidates.[18] Catholic clergy now played an important role at these conventions as well as in many cases, such as in Co. Westmeath,[19] providing local leadership for national league branches. In the months immediately preceding the election, candidates were selected for every constituency, except those Ulster divisions with a protestant majority. So successful was the party in capturing the nationalist electorate that only in one Irish constituency did an independent nationalist stand. In early October Parnell declared that the party platform would

consist of a single plank, 'the plank of legislative independence'.[20]

In response to this nationalist reorganisation the Irish loyal
and patriotic union was formed in Dublin in May 1885 by a
number of southern businessmen, landowners and academics. It sought to organise opposition in the three southern
provinces to the nationalists, and to unite liberals and conservatives on a common platform of maintenance of the
union. The Irish loyal and patriotic union also published
pamphlets and leaflets which were circulated widely. In its
aim of bringing together liberals and conservatives the
I.L.P.U. was successful, and in some cases candidates came
forward in the election simply as 'loyalists'. A total of 54 of the
southern seats were contested by anti-home rule candidates.[21]

In Ulster, however, appeals for unity between supporters of
the union went unheeded and the liberal and conservative
parties continued to operate separately. The election of 1885
in Ulster involved not only nationalists against supporters of
the union but rivalry between liberal and conservative.
Before the general election, the Ulster liberals, whose support lay chiefly with the tenant farmers, and included both
catholics and presbyterians, held nine seats. With an impressive headquarters at the recently built Reform Club in Belfast,
they sought to develop new local divisional associations. In
spite of a good central office, however, and contrary to later
claims of a strong liberal effort, the evidence of liberal activity at the registration courts and in the constituencies during
the campaign reflected lack of vitality and effective local
organisation.[22] Attempts were made to embrace labourers in
their new divisional associations, though with little success,
partly because of the identification of the liberals with the
farmers' cause. On the eve of the 1885 general election, the
liberals still retained considerable support among presbyterian farmers even if it was clear that the nationalist movement
was proving very attractive to catholic farmers in Ulster who
had formerly voted liberal. Liberal candidates declared their
support for the union between Great Britain and Ireland and
also called for further land reform.

Before the 1885 general election the conservatives held 17 seats in Ulster. They were widely regarded as the former land-lord party, and because of this their electoral prospects must have appeared poor. Conservative party organisation had developed to some extent in the province over the previous ten years with the growth of a number of county and borough conservative associations, but these bodies had a limited pop-ular involvement. Historians have sometimes painted a bleak picture of conservative organisation during 1885, but this pic-ture relies on the evidence of party apathy and disunity in Counties Armagh and Fermanagh.[23] Elsewhere, however, matters were very different, especially in the north-east of Ulster. Under the energetic leadership of E. S. Finnigan, a full-time party organiser based in Belfast, the conservatives extensively reorganised in 1885. Finnigan helped to set up, with strong local participation, many divisional associations, especially in the key areas of Belfast and Counties Antrim and Down.[24]

A vital aspect of these new branches was the involvement of the Orange Order. Local lodges were given special positions in many of the new organisations. Speaking, for example, in Ballynahinch, Co. Down, on 7 May 1885, Finnigan described proposals to set up a broadly based local committee: 'The Orange Association would have a well defined position. The district master and district officers ... would be appointed ... upon each committee'.[25] At this stage the Order was a minor-ity movement among protestants, but it embraced many of the newly enfranchised labourers and was therefore an important means of integrating the working-class into the conservative party. Such arrangements went smoothly in Counties Antrim and Down, but ran into trouble in Belfast and counties Armagh and Londonderry, where Orange labourers felt that they were being given no influence in the new conservative machine: in the latter areas they rebelled against the local conservative organisers and either forced them to accept candidates agreeable to them or, as in the case of two of the four Belfast seats, ran independent candidates of their own. In a number of cases in addition, conservative party organisers co-operated secretly with nationalist party organisers to undermine the liberals and the middle ground. Conservative candidates emphasised their support for the union.

In Ulster the nationalist party had started the election campaign in a weak position. Only three of the former Ulster MPs were home rulers, thanks to a weak home rule organisation in the past and to the success of the Ulster liberals in attracting the anti-conservative vote. During 1885, however, the National League expanded considerably in many parts of Ulster. A government report on National League activity over the period 1 January – 30 June 1885 commented: 'the most noteworthy feature is the progress that the League is making in Ulster, especially in Armagh, Down, Fermanagh, Tyrone and Monaghan; three new branches have even been started in Co. Antrim'.[26] League organisers from Dublin, such as Timothy Harrington, played an important role in the spread of the movement and in its preparations for the elections. Conventions, under the chairmanship of a representative of the party leadership, were held to select candidates for those constituencies with a catholic majority. Mid-Armagh was the only division with a protestant majority contested by a nationalist (see paragraph below). In both the conventions and the National League branches, catholic clergy played an important part in most constituencies. Only in Co. Londonderry was there an effort, among both clergy and party leaders, to avoid a clerical image.[27]

Early in the campaign strong efforts were made to promote nationalist unity. National League branches in Belfast, favourable to Michael Davitt, were closed down in late 1884 and early 1885, and other steps were taken to weaken his influence, including the removal of the editor of the *Morning News*, C. J. Dempsey, a supporter of Davitt's, who later commented to John Pinkerton 'I am too great a disciple of Davitt's ... the MPs want me effaced from Ulster politics'.[28] In some areas nationalist organisers co-operated secretly with conservative organisers to keep all catholics together in the nationalist movement and also to undermine the liberals. For example, to thwart Dempsey standing for South Armagh, the local convention under the chairmanship of T.M. Healy had picked a compromise candidate, Alex Blane, a tailor by trade. Since in Healy's words, 'nobody knew him and snobbery was rampant,' this aroused the threat of an independent nation- alist splitting the catholic vote, a danger only averted by Healy secretly arranging for a conservative to come forward in South Armagh, which obliged the independent to step down; in return for this conservative favour, Healy agreed to put for- ward a nationalist candidate in Mid-Armagh to damage the liberal candidate's chances.[29] In other areas where there was no nationalist candidate, the catholic vote was given to the conservatives to help destroy the liberals and any potential cross-community electoral support they might command.[30]

The outcome of the election was a resounding victory for the nationalist party which won 85 seats throughout Ireland, plus a seat in Liverpool; in Ulster the party held 17 out of the 33 constituencies. Apart from two Dublin University seats, held by the conservatives, pro-union candidates were suc- cessful only in Ulster, where the conservative party took 16 seats while the liberal party failed to win a single division. These conservative figures include two successful indepen- dent candidates in Belfast who were subsequently adopted by the official conservative associations. Out of 85 nationalists, 80 were catholic; all Ulster nationalist M.P.s were catholic. All the 19 conservatives were members of the Church of Ireland, except for three presbyterians and one methodist; most of the unsuccessful liberals had been presbyterian. Parnell now returned to parliament with a strong, disciplined nationalist party. For their part, the Ulster conservatives had emerged as the clear leaders of pro-union support in Ireland.

An analysis of the voting for the two sides shows a high degree of religious polarisation in the constituencies. It is clear that nearly all catholics who voted backed the national- ist party, except in some northern constituencies where there were no nationalist candidates and where catholics voted conservative for tactical reasons. In perhaps as many as six divisions last minute catholic support for the conservative against the liberal proved significant.[31] In a few southern con- stituencies small numbers of catholics may have voted for pro-union candidates. It is also evident that nearly all protestants who voted supported pro-union candidates. Although protestants were 10 per cent of the population outside Ulster, they were too widely dispersed to win any seats. In Co. Londonderry there is evidence of some protestants voting for a nationalist, (partly because of the candidate's reputation on the land question, and efforts in the county to present a non-sectarian image). Generally, however, it is clear that the electorate had polarised sharply along denominational lines throughout the country. Protestant nationalists such as C.S. Parnell, or Jeremiah Jordan from Co. Fermanagh, and catholic unionists such as Daniel O'Connell, son of the Liberator, and W.T. McGrath from Belfast were rare exceptions.

Within nine months there occurred another general election, which would serve to copperfasten the outcome of the 1885 general election. Early in 1886 Gladstone announced his support for home rule, and in April the first home rule bill was introduced but defeated. Gladstone's action now caused a split among the liberals. In Ulster the vast majority of liberals became liberal unionists and in the general election of mid 1886 joined with the conservatives in a common pro-union front. Various social and denominational differences between the former liberals and conservatives were ignored in the new unionist movement. A small group of pro-Gladstone supporters fought the election as Gladstonian liberals. There also appeared a new organisation called the Irish protestant home rule association with the aim of promoting the principle of home rule among protestants.[32]

At the 1886 general election only 33 constituencies in Ireland were contested, compared with 79 in 1885; outside Ulster a mere seven divisions out of 68 saw a poll. Out of 70 nationalist candidates, 62 were returned unopposed in the southern provinces: the eight who were opposed were returned with large majorities. Most Ulster divisions were contested.[33] In 17 of these contests, conservatives faced nationalists (including some protestant nationalist candidates) in five, liberal unionists fought nationalists and in another five Gladstonian liberals opposed conservatives. The bulk of former liberals in the main unionist constituencies in

the north-east played little active part in the election, leaving
the unionist political organisations to be effectively controlled by the conservative victors of 1885. The outcome in
Ulster was the election of 15 conservatives, 2 liberal unionists
and 16 nationalists. Overall, the nationalists won 84 seats,
plus a seat in Liverpool. The conservatives won 17 (including
two Dublin University seats) and the liberal unionists 2, a
result which reflected accurately the comparative strength of
the two groups in the new unionist movement.

Viewed broadly, it is evident that again most catholic voters
supported nationalist candidates and most protestant voters
backed unionist candidates. Some protestants did vote for
nationalists, although it is difficult to put a precise figure on
their numbers. Probably it is fair to say that only around 3,000
protestants (mainly former liberals) voted for Gladstonian
liberals and nationalist candidates. Under the unionist flag
were now both former conservatives and liberals. The latter
would survive as a minor grouping within the unionist family
until the full incorporation of the Ulster Liberal Unionist
Society into the unionist party in 1911. The nationalist party
would split over the Parnell divorce but eventually would suc-
ceed in realigning itself within the broad framework established in 1885. These two crucial years, therefore, saw the
emergence of nationalism and unionism in Ireland and the
polarisation of politics on the basis of religious affiliation. In
spite of later attempts at accommodation the divisions that
emerged at this time with catholic and nationalist on one side
and protestant and unionist on the other remained central to
Irish politics up to 1921 and formed a basic background to
the politics that emerged thereafter.

III

The political developments of 1885–6 had a vital effect on
how nationalism and unionism emerged finally in their particular forms. These two years were the climax to a period of
great political change and mobilisation in the whole country.
The extension of the franchise and changes in electoral law,
as well as the high degree of popular excitement over the

issues that now held the public attention, meant that entirely new demands were placed on party organisations and leaders. Their response to this situation not only affected immediate party fortunes but also influenced greatly the whole nature of politics to emerge at this time. The structure and spirit of the new party organisations had a very important bearing on the type of politics and society to develop. These parties reflected certain divisions in society, and particular elements (such as the Orange Order and the catholic clergy) had key roles in the new organisational structures. The religious divisions in Irish society had often had some bearing on party divisions but in 1885-6 the two victorious parties based firmly their respective movements on denominational differences. The decisions by both the nationalist and conservative party leadership to adapt their organisations in the way they did (important in the first instance to meet the challenges of 1885–6 and to win the elections) had a far-reaching influence on the new political and social confrontations which materialised at these elections.

Many special features of nationalism and unionism were the result of developments which occurred in these years. The new nationalist movement that emerged had support from throughout the island of Ireland, but in practice it represented only the catholic community.[34] The events of this period ensured that Irish nationalism emerged as a catholic movement with strong clerical support. There had been connections in the past between Irish nationalism and catholicism but events of the mid-1880s established the link in a formal and thorough way. Ironically, it was a protestant leader of the nationalist party, C.S. Parnell, who was responsible for the 'alliance' of 1884–5 between nationalism and the catholic church in Ireland which played a vital part in the electoral success of his party in 1885. Undoubtedly, as Professor Emmet Larkin has argued, this link had democratic benefits in that it prevented the emergence of an all-powerful central party,[35] but it did help to give Irish nationalism a strong denominational character.

The new unionist movement was concerned with defending the union but because of the events of 1885–6 it represented only protestants and won seats only in Ulster. The failure of the Ulster liberals to hold catholic support meant that the new combination of former liberals and con- servatives represented just one part of the Ulster population. This new unionist movement, furthermore, was dominated by the conservative, Orange-backed element in Ulster society, with the gentry still prominent, at the expense of the more radical, liberal section. Ironically, the tactical support given by nationalists to conservative candidates in 1885 played a vital role in moving power in the pro-union community to conservative elements. The link between the Orange lodges and the new unionist associations did introduce a populist, democratic element into unionist politics but it also served to reinforce the denominational nature of unionism. The indi- vidual responsible for this Orange/Unionist link was E.S. Finnigan and not, as is often alleged, Lord Randolph Churchill, whose well-known 'Orange card' speech was made only in 1886 (after the link was well established) and related primarily to English power politics. Outside of Ulster, union- ists formed an important minority but their only parliamen- tary representation came from the two Dublin University seats.

The 1885–6 general elections marked the birth of modern politics in both parts of Ireland.[36] In the succeeding three and a half decades up to 1923 there would be significant developments which would affect the new territorial and con- stitutional arrangements to emerge in the early 1920s, but which would not alter the essentials of the conflict that mate- rialised in 1885-6. Unionism would move from a concern to maintain all Ireland for the union, to a defence of Ulster, and then to support for only six of the Ulster counties. Nationalism would witness the collapse of the parliamentary nationalist party and the triumph of Sinn Fein. Support from the main parties in Britain affected the fortunes of both nationalists and unionists. The threat or use of violence played an important role. The two new states would be marked by the turmoil of their establishment in the years 1920–3. All these developments, however, took place within the basic framework established in 1885-6 and served to modify but not to replace the fundamental confrontations and alliances which emerged at that time. The results of the 1918 general election served only to confirm the outcome of these crucial earlier general elections.

Conflict over nationalism remained the key factor, whether between nationalist and unionist before 1921, between pro-treaty and anti-treaty nationalists in the Irish civil war or between unionists and nationalists in Northern Ireland after 1921. The new party systems to emerge in both the Irish Free State and Northern Ireland were greatly influenced by this conflict, which effectively diminished the importance of other social and regional divisions. The connection between politics and religious division remained very strong. Both sides could sometimes win supporters across the denominational barriers such as the catholic unionist M.P. Denis Henry, or the protestant Sinn Féin M.P. and T.D., Ernest Blythe. Nonetheless, unionism and nationalism were rooted firmly in their respective religious camps. After 1921 most protestants in the south were politically marginalised outside the main parties, while in the north political and religious divisions remained strongly linked. The creation of two new political units in Ireland in 1921, and the political systems 'without social bases', that emerged in both parts thereafter, are directly linked to the outcome of the 1885–6 general elections.

IV

Why were these elections so important? Other elections in the nineteenth century had witnessed significant events, but none had such obvious lasting relevance. Part of the answer to this question lies in the nature of some of the broader changes that occurred. Key social and economic developments, in particular the main resolution of the land question, the enormous growth of Belfast and the strengthening of religious identities, all of which set the scene for modern Ireland, occurred in the preceding period. This, it should also be remembered, was the era when for the first time the vast majority of the people were able to read and write.

The other part of the answer lies in the very significant extension of the franchise and the rise of modern political parties
that took place in these years of mass political mobilisation
and electoral change. Although universal suffrage was still a
thing of the future, most households had a vote. There was
now an extensive network of local political associations with
popular involvement, and, especially in the nationalist case, a
strong central party organisation.

The importance of such developments has been noted
elsewhere by political scientists.[37] In many parts of Europe the
particular divisions that emerged as important at the end of
the nineteenth and the beginning of the twentieth centuries
have remained significant throughout the succeeding years.
Party systems have continued remarkably true to the traditions and shape of the politics established at this point where
broad-based modern parties, with a wide franchise, came into
being for the first time. People have subsequently voted simply for the same parties as their parents. Even when particular parties have collapsed and new ones have arisen, they have
often remained within the basic framework of the party
system established at this earlier stage. Nationalism and
unionism, along with religious divisions, emerged at this
key formative period to dominate modern politics in
Ireland.

Neither the polarisation of politics along denominational
lines nor the emergence of nationalism were unique to
Ireland, but have strong parallels in contemporary Europe.
Although it was no longer a major factor in politics in Great
Britain by this stage, religious conflict remained important in
other parts of Western Europe. In Germany, Switzerland and
Holland there were significant divisions between protestant
and catholic parties.[38] Various European countries, such as
Norway and Italy, also experienced the rise of nationalist politics with important consequences for party cleavages.[39] The
situation in Ireland, however, differed from the situation in
these countries in that, besides religious differences, there
was also a split over the national question and, because of the
changes we have witnessed, each division powerfully reinforced the other.

These elections of 1885–6, then, saw the emergence of two distinct political movements, based firmly on particular religious groupings, with strongly opposed views on the nature of the nation, the state and the central issue of sovereignty. Both sides would claim ancient historical roots for their position, but in fact the conflict that emerged was greatly influenced by contemporary political and social developments. At this key period, party leaders, organisers and supporters, influenced and aided by the social, economic and religious developments of their age, created a new order of politics where the religious and national divisions were firmly related in a form that would prove long-lasting. Later political events would influence the final territorial and constitutional shape of the new political units to emerge in 1921 but the outcome of the events surrounding the general elections of 1885 and 1886 decided the basic character of political conflict in the country. These crucial years set the scene for the rivalry between unionist and nationalist in the north and between different nationalist groups in the south which has dominated all subsequent political development in both parts of Ireland.

3

RELIGION AND POLITICS: IRISH PROBLEMS AND EUROPEAN COMPARISONS

Most people would accept that religion is very relevant to the politics of Northern Ireland. Few reports on the situation fail to mention divisions between protestants and catholics. Often our problems are seen as the products of a unique history: the conflicts are a hangover from the religious wars of the seventeenth century, whereas people in other countries are now having to cope with more modern types of problems, such as class politics. Frequently, however, the struggle over religion is seen as a cover for other conflicts, such as competition for land or resources, and it is argued that theology has little to do with the actual situation. To gain an understanding of how important religion *really* is, it is instructive to look at matters in a European context. The religious wars of the seventeenth century with their consequences for Ireland are well known but few people in either Great Britain or Ireland are aware of connections between religion and politics in Western Europe in the twentieth century. Such a study may help to determine to what extent our situation is unusual, and exactly how important religion is.

I

To begin with, it will be useful to describe in more detail the arguments for and against religion being an important factor in the present situation. Some argue that religion and religious divisions in our community are not really very significant. It is claimed often that the sectarian differences in society are actually based on things other than religion - social differences, national differences or other matters. Sir Kenneth Bloomfield, former head of the Northern Ireland Civil Service, has written in his memoirs that 'religion was the identifying mark of the division in Northern Ireland, but not its essence ... The central dispute was not about religion, but about power'.[1] James O'Connell of the Department of Peace Studies, University of Bradford, has agreed:

> If this Irish conflict is not about religion, it is organised around Christian allegiances, and it is worsened by religious bitterness. It is in its essence a struggle for political power; and it is nourished by the fears of two minority groups, one a minority in Ireland and the other a minority in Northern Ireland.[2]

Another academic commentator, the political scientist Jürg Steiner has declared:

> In Northern Ireland, the problem appears on the surface to be a religious one, and the mass media usually speak of civil strife between protestants and catholics. But, below the surface, the battle is really between two ethnic groups, the British and the Irish. The former happen to be protestants and the latter, catholics, but the conflict is not primarily about religious matters, although the purely religious dimension has some importance too. But essentially it is much more a struggle between two cultures unwilling to share the same territory.[3]

It has also been argued that religion is important only because certain people have exploited it to their own advantage. Some socialists have claimed that the bosses have used religious conflict to keep the workers divided. Marxist interpretations of the situation in Northern Ireland have

downplayed the religious dimension.[4] Many nationalists and
republicans believe that religion is only significant because it
has been exploited by the British government to keep Irish
people apart. In 1921 Michael Collins remarked: 'as to religious intolerance, this was the product solely and entirely of
English policy operating in Ireland'.[5] Some unionists also
believe that our conflict has little to do with religion. Lord
Ernest Hamilton, writing in 1917, put forward his belief that
if the problem was 'merely religious', then 'a gradual incline
towards tolerance from both sides might be hoped for'.[6] For
him religion was simply a badge to mark opposite sides in a
struggle between different races and nationalities over the
basic issue of territory. Sir Basil Brooke in 1934 insisted that
the conflict was not about religion but about loyalty to the
state.[7] The modern historian A.T.Q. Stewart has commented
about the situation in Northern Ireland:

> The exact cause of the quarrel, or more accurately of its survival,
> is often obscure to the onlooker. In many countries it is assumed
> that it is a holy war, *al jihad, Konfessionskrieg*, and as such an ab-
> normality in modernised societies, a sickening survival of a
> mediaeval religious rancour. The fact is, however, that the
> quarrel is not about theology as such and remains, in its modern
> form, stubbornly a constitutional problem, though religion is the
> shibboleth of the contending parties. Essentially the conflict in
> Ulster is not different from other conflicts in the modern world:
> it is about political power and who should wield it.[8]

In opposition to this, however, there are others who argue
that religion is very important. This view is found particularly
among many northern protestants, who see the conflict in
Northern Ireland as a deep-seated religious conflict between
protestantism and Roman catholicism. A number of opinion
surveys have shown that for many protestants the catholic
church is seen as the main threat. In a local survey in 1993,
Sister Rose Devlin from Draperstown, Co. Londonderry,
found opposition from protestants to cross community
efforts because of this religious concern: 'The Roman
Catholic Church is feared as a monolithic organisation, [is]

seen as subverting the protestant faith and imposing a
catholic social order... as one interviewee put it, "the protestant community knows that it is in a minority in Ireland and
it feels threatened."[9] In a talk to the Dublin Rotary Club in
early April 1995, Mr John Taylor gave three reasons why people in Northern Ireland are unionist: the first is loyalty to the
crown, the second is the financial advantage of belonging to
the UK, while the third is 'an in-built fear of the Church of
Rome', which he described as 'a strong factor in Northern
Ireland, one [that] must not be underestimated'.[10]

Some even go as far as to see this religious division as a fundamental one which affects all aspects of life, and over which
there can be no compromise. Professor Steve Bruce, in his
book on protestant fundamentalism in Northern Ireland, has
argued that some see the situation as a basic religious conflict, between good and evil, between right and wrong, and
one in which there can only be one winner.[11] This view is
found especially among followers of the Democratic Unionist
Party. At a D.U.P. conference in 1991 Councillor Roy
Gillespie from Ballymena stated that 'The Roman Catholic
church is the problem in our province' and that 'Rome's aim
is to destroy protestantism, our children, our children's children, our way of life and the Bible.'[12] In their submission to
the Forum for Peace and Reconciliation in Dublin, April
1995, members of the Evangelical Contribution on Northern
Ireland stressed this religious concern.[13] Mr David McMillan
stated that for some northern protestants, the Roman
Catholic church epitomised everything that was 'evil and
anti-Christian': for them the reformation was still alive, and to
accommodate - even fraternise with - catholics was to sign
your own death warrant. Mr David Porter said that the fear of
Rome was very substantial and that it underlay the political
views of many northern protestants.

II

Who is correct? Is religion, and the conflict over religion,
really important for the politics of our community? To make
some sense of this debate it will be helpful to look at politics
in Western Europe in the twentieth century. A number of

political scientists have examined in depth the politics of the
countries of Western Europe and their findings make interesting reading. Professor Richard Rose and Professor Derek
Unwin have remarked on the subject: 'Religion, not class, is
the main social basis of parties in the western world today'.[14]
This comment was based on observations on politics, not in
the 1660s nor the 1860s but in the late 1960s. These words
appeared in an analysis of parties and their electoral support
in seventeen different democratic countries, of which thirteen were in Western Europe. They considered the effect on
party politics of a wide range of divisions such as those created by class, religion and nationalism. They concluded that
a total of 35 parties in 11 different countries were cohesive
because of a common religious or anti-religious outlook
among their supporters. The picture that emerged clearly
was that religion mattered more than any other single variable in the greatest number of parties.

It has been observed that there are three patterns of religious balance to be found in Western Europe: the mainly
catholic countries, those with approximate catholic and
protestant parity, and those which are largely protestant.[15] It
is in the catholic countries that religion has had the most
direct political connection; among the reasons given for this
are the wide social claims of catholicism, its hierarchical
structure and its frequent conflict with nationalist and socialist movements. This has led to anticlericalism, and to accompanying strong divisions between clerical and anticlerical
groups and between churchgoing and non-churchgoing
catholics, frequently resulting in the emergence of Christian
Democratic parties, which have as their original purpose the
defence of catholic values in politics, often in connection
with the control of education. This has been especially true in
Italy, Austria, Belgium and Luxembourg.

In Italy, for example, there has been a firm alliance
between the Christian Democratic Party and the catholic
church; opposed to them are socialists and communists who
are found most strongly among atheists or non-churchgoing
catholics, although at the last general election catholic intervention has been more diffuse among parties, thanks to the

collapse of the global communist threat. Religious issues rarely come up directly in the politics of most of these countries today but religious values and background (churchgoing or non-churchgoing) remain important determinants in voting preferences. Christian Democratic parties, now well established in various political systems, continue to maintain a strong role in Western European politics. In the European parliament the Christian Democratic parties make up the second largest grouping, called the European People's Party, with the subtitle 'Federation of Christian Democratic Parties of the EC.'

In some countries the catholic church has been so powerful that anti-clericalism has featured rarely. This is true of Spain and Portugal where the dictatorial régimes of the two countries prevented anticlericalism. These dictatorships have now gone, but in the new circumstances of the last two decades, with very different church state relations, strong clericalism or anticlericalism have failed to take root in a major way. In the republic of Ireland, Professor Gordon Smith states that, uniquely among democratic countries of Western Europe, the catholic church had 'almost unquestioned supremacy' and faced 'a complete absence of anticlericalism despite occasions when the catholic hierarchy actively intervened in politics'.[16]

Next we look at those countries with important protestant/catholic divisions, namely the Netherlands, Switzerland and Germany.[17] The Netherlands has a catholic population of 40 per cent. Until the mid-1970s there were three large confessional parties. The catholic vote went predominantly to the Catholic People's Party while the protestant vote was divided among two main parties, the Anti-Revolutionary Party and the Christian Historical Union. Until the 1960s the total religious vote was over 50 per cent. There were other non-confessional parties – labour and liberal. These three groups, the catholic party, the two protestant parties and the labour and liberal section formed what were called the 'pillars' of Dutch society with their own unions, schools and other organisations. During the twentieth century various alliances of these groups were formed to create the Dutch government. Then in 1976, in face of a growing secular threat the Christian Democratic Appeal was formed out of the three religious groups and is today the largest single party in the Netherlands.

In Switzerland catholics are also a minority of approximately 41 per cent. Much power in the country is devolved to local cantons many of which are segregated fairly closely on religious grounds. The federal government is run by a national council headed by a permanent coalition, in both of which the Christian Democrats' People's Party (formerly the Catholic People's Party) drawing support largely from the catholic electors, is a major partner: the protestant vote is split among various other parties. No longer as important as it was in the nineteenth and early twentieth centuries, religious division survives as one of several important variables in voting in Switzerland.

In Germany under the Imperial government and during the Weimar republic religion remained an important factor in politics. In a country where protestants were a substantial majority, the Catholic Centre Party retained strong catholic support. With the collapse of the party system under the Nazis and the partition of Germany in 1945, which separated the predominantly protestant east from the rest of Germany and led to approximate catholic/protestant parity in west Germany, a new party system emerged. The Christian Democratic Union which was established at this stage in West Germany was based to a considerable extent on the church-going catholic population with some protestant support. Some smaller conservative parties also attracted protestant votes. With the collapse of these smaller parties and a broadening of the Christian Democratic base, however, the denominational differences have come to mean a lot less to present day voters. Following re-unification there has been an upsurge of support in the area of the former East Germany for the Christian Democrats, whose catholic/Christian origins are seen as preferable to those of other parties with left wing backgrounds.

Lastly, we come to those countries with a substantial protestant majority, namely Britain and the Scandinavian countries.

In the twentieth century there has been less connection between voting behaviour and religion in these states than in the other groups of European countries. This is because the protestant churches have never been so tightly knit socially nor so co-operative in spirit that they have been able to override their differences for any length of time.[18] In the nineteenth century, British politics were still rooted in religion.[19] By the twentieth century, however, in spite of some issues such as disestablishment of the Welsh episcopalian church and the controversy over church schools, religion has no longer determined in a significant way political loyalties in Great Britain.

Since the 1960s religious practice has declined in the western world and religious division is not so important as it once was to European political life. Yet, as a perceptive French observer commented in 1987 in his book *Government and politics in Western Europe* 'the influence of religion endures, as if the values connected with it persisted and were directing political behaviour despite the decline of religious practice and the weakening of institutional allegiances.'[20] It has been argued that a weakening of religious practice will lead to the decline of the religious vote. Other analyses, however, have emphasised a continuity of political behaviour thanks to the survival of religious values at the centre of European societies, despite the decline of the institutional churches, and because of the ability of the older religious parties to adapt to new circumstances.[21] At the same time, the formation of religious parties in some countries of Eastern Europe and the appearance of a fundamentalist electorate in North America may herald the revival of a religious vote.

The picture from Western Europe, therefore, gives us a valuable perspective on this question of the importance of religion. The evidence from many countries shows that religion can be a very real political factor, not an artifice. Nowhere in Western Europe where there are societies divided between protestant and catholic has there not been a serious political problem and in various other predominantly catholic countries religion has provided a very significant element in politics. Religion is relevant to politics as an ideology, as a belief and value system with important roots not merely in the sixteenth century but in the late nineteenth and early twentieth centuries when our modern political systems emerged. Denominational and religious consciousness has proved just as important as class or nationalist consciousness in creating and maintaining political awareness and political parties in our contemporary twentieth-century world. So the argument of those protestants who claim that religion is a pertinent factor in our situation has considerable validity when the broader picture is studied.

However, there are two qualifications which must be made of this viewpoint, and the evidence from the same Western European arena provides the substance for them. First, while religion is undoubtedly very important, other factors cannot be ignored, such as nationalist, class or language divisions; secondly, serious as these religious divisions frequently are, people elsewhere have found means to accommodate or deal with such differences. As regards the first point, various political scientists have emphasised that the importance of a particular division depends considerably on its relationship with other divisions: the *combination* of division is very significant.[22] In Switzerland, for example, there is an important cleavage over religion and another division over language, but these divisions do not strengthen each other since both German speaking and French speaking is found among both protestants and catholics. This helps to moderate the religious division. In Holland there has been a sharp division between protestant and catholic, but the other major division in Holland of class has not reinforced this because the working classes and middle classes are distributed equally among both groups. Also in Holland and Switzerland a common sense of nationality helps to bind people together.

So while religion is a crucial division in these societies, other matters are influential in deciding precisely what the effect of this division will be. On the one hand, dividing factors such as those arising over language or class are distributed equally in these countries and do not serve to reinforce the religious division. On the other hand, certain factors are shared by both sides and help to moderate conflict. A common sense of nationality helps to minimise potential confrontation arising out of the religious division. Those who argue that religion is all important fail to realise how relevant these other cleavages can be. When we turn to look at Northern Ireland, we see that the relationship between religious and other divisions is different from those in countries such as Holland and Switzerland, and this special circumstance has a significant influence.

In Northern Ireland, other important divisions reinforce the religious cleavage. While class structure is distributed fairly equally between the two sides at present, in the past there have been inequalities of jobs and wealth and there are still problems, as seen, for instance, in the higher rate of catholic unemployment. In earlier times, catholics have had less access to the corridors of power and influence than protestants. There are some reinforcing cultural divisions over issues like the Irish language, in spite of efforts to make the language available to all. Above all, however, conflict over political allegiance, between nationalists on the one side and unionists on the other, over the questions of the constitutional position and legitimacy of the state, largely correlates to, and reinforces, the religious cleavage. The community in Northern Ireland lacks a common sense of nationality or community which could help to mitigate the religious differences and create society wide loyalties. However, even when taking these factors into account, we must nevertheless remember that religious division remains crucial to our society, as it has to many other European communities. Those who believe that religion is important often do not appreciate these other factors, while those who downgrade the religious factor, often give them too much importance.

The second qualification which must be made regarding the problem of religion is that while religious division is usually very significant for politics, the matter can be coped with successfully. As has been demonstrated in other European countries, this division can be 'accommodated': compromise is possible and people can live peacefully together regardless of these differences.[23] In the Netherlands, in spite of sharp differences which have strongly influenced party political life

from at least the beginning of the century, the opposing confessional parties have been willing to co-operate to provide
effective government for the community. Indeed, common
interests over education gave a special impetus to this in the
early decades of the twentieth century. Coalition governments, often containing members from both religious sides,
have run the country. Yet in spite of this co-operation, the
religious parties retained separate identities up to 1976.
Brought together in a new party in that year, in order to promote their cause in an increasingly secular world, the two religious sides are still regularly in government.

In both Germany and Switzerland, in spite of deep denominational divisions in the past, parties have been able to operate across the religious divide. Their success in doing so,
especially in the last half of the twentieth century, should not
allow us to forget the depth of this conflict and its effect on
politics in the previous period. It is interesting to note the
composition of the present-day Christian Democratic group
in the European parliament. While having its origins in
mainly catholic interests, the Christian Democrats, now the
second largest group in the parliament, have achieved
a much broader basis. They include Dutch Christian
Democrats from the former protestant and catholic parties
and also German Christian Democrats from both protestant
and catholic sections of the reunited country.

Another point to note about many Western European
countries which have successfully dealt with deep divisions,
religious or otherwise, is that accommodation has been made
possible by using types of governments and political representation which provide democratic government but often
do not employ the majority government system as seen at
Westminster. In countries such as the Netherlands and
Switzerland other forms of government, including coalitions,
federal councils, referendums and bills of rights for minori-
ties, are adopted to accommodate differences. Straight
majority rule might leave groups permanently excluded, and
so methods of government have been specially devised to
prevent this. Some of the practices are laid down in law, while
others have developed through voluntary agreements.

For example, in Switzerland the main parties normally invite representatives of the smaller parties to join them in the federal government. At the same time, we should realise that certain conditions are necessary for these 'consociational' structures to survive such as a genuine will to preserve the system, the ability of groups to accept compromise and the skill of leaders 'to prepare and organise political solutions rather than exacerbate conflicts and passions'.[24]

The evidence from the European picture, then, is clearly that religion can be a real dividing factor in the politics of a society. Why is this point not appreciated more widely? Explaining the incomprehension of English people about this religious conflict, Ronald McNeill (later Lord Cushendun) wrote in 1922 of 'the astonishing shortness of their memory in regard to their own history and their very limited outlook on the world outside their own island.'[25] Here he referred to the strong 'no popery' sentiment in mid-Victorian England and to the bitter clerical/anticlerical feeling in contemporary France, which English people either forgot or ignored. During the twentieth century religion declined rapidly as an important variable in the politics of nearly all parts of Great Britain, so that today it no longer figures in analyses of general elections, and many books on politics in contemporary Britain carry no reference to religion in their indexes. British interest in European politics is still very limited. Many British political studies and textbooks on Europe concentrate on the large European countries, such as France and Germany, rather than the smaller ones, like Switzerland and the Netherlands, where one tends to find religious cleavage and forms of government different to those of the United Kingdom, and they also pay special attention to issues such as fascism rather than religious factors. For these reasons, most people in Great Britain are still unable to grasp that religion can be a real political problem for many societies in our modern world.

Among the population of the Republic of Ireland there is also little comprehension of the importance of the religious dimension to the conflict within Northern Ireland and between north and south. Many southerners will deny the validity of unionist fears over religion or will acknowledge them only as 'perceived' or 'imaginary'. In contrast to Great Britain, where religion has ceased to be relevant to politics, with the result that British people cannot understand why it is important elsewhere, in the Republic of Ireland religion remains so integral to society that the majority of southerners often fail to appreciate either its significance to their own community or why northern unionists should see the south as a religious threat. Commenting on the importance of religion in the republic, Professor Gordon Smith has remarked on how 'religious values [have] permeated state and society; only recently has the role of religion in public and private life been questioned seriously.'[26] Another matter of importance in the southern lack of understanding of the religious factor is the position of a number of protestants among Irish nationalist leaders, such as Wolfe Tone and C.S. Parnell, which leads many nationalists to deny the element of religious conflict in the situation, in spite of the evidence of the underlying reality of this sectarian dimension.

As an example of this unwillingness in the south to recognise the reality of the religious dimension we may note the events surrounding the proposal to create a new national library of Ireland, 1959–60, which Dr John Bowman has investigated in a recent article.[27] In November 1962, Mr C.J. Haughey, the republic's minister for justice, at a student debate at Queen's University Belfast, sought to reassure protestants that they had no reason to fear religious intolerance in a united Ireland: he asserted that unionist fears about the power of the catholic church were groundless. Yet just over three years previously when a proposal was put to the taoiseach, Séan Lemass, that a new national library should be created from the existing national library of Ireland and the library at Trinity College, it was privately referred to the catholic archbishop of Dublin, John Charles McQuade, for his comments. When he strongly rejected the proposal because he thought that it would benefit Trinity and that the 'chief university institution in a mainly catholic community should manifestly be a catholic institution,' the scheme was dropped without protest. In spite of this, a decade later

Lemass would say that he could not recollect any occasion 'when the church tried to pressure me in an area affecting government policy.'

III

It will be helpful to remind ourselves of the extent of the connection between religion and politics in Ireland, north and south, over the last century. Before the general elections of 1885–6 there had been links between the two, but there had also been occasions when the catholic hierarchy sought to avoid clerical involvement in politics and when voting patterns among protestants crossed denominational boundaries. In the mid-1880s, however, religion and politics became firmly linked among the greatly extended electorate and in the political forms of unionism and nationalism which appeared at this time. The clear emergence of religion in politics was by no means unique to Ireland; in fact, as Professor Norman Stone has pointed out, in many other countries in Western Europe in the 1880s, such as Italy and Belgium, where an extension of the suffrage similar to that in Ireland also occurred, parties based on a clerical/catholic voter alliance emerged to play a key political role.[28] Of particular significance for Ireland, however, was the special link between religious division and the nationalist/unionist conflict which developed in these years.

During the mid-1880s, following the nationalist party's endorsement of separate catholic education and concerned that the party might become a revolutionary movement, the catholic church obtained a key role in the organisational structures of the new nationalist movement under the leadership of C.S. Parnell. Catholic clergy gave vital leadership to local branches of the movement and played an important role in the selection of M.P.s. Writing in September 1885, Archbishop W.J. Walsh of Dublin, commented: 'I have got the position of the priests recognised as *priests* in the county conventions for the selection of M.P.s'.[29] The nationalist movement swept the polls, but only among the catholic electorate. This clerical involvement would be a central feature of nationalist politics in late nineteenth and early twentieth century Ireland.

A new revolutionary republican movement developed in the twentieth century and by 1918 had taken over from the old nationalist party. In spite of conflict between some of these republicans and catholic bishops over the use of violence and in spite of the presence of a few protestant Sinn Féin MPs in 1918, such as Ernest Blythe, M.P. for North Monaghan, the new movement remained firmly rooted in the catholic community. Professor Tom Garvin has shown how for many of these revolutionaries their catholicism was an essential part of their political identity.[30] Shortly before his execution in 1916 the revolutionary socialist James Connolly was not only received back into the catholic church but also persuaded his protestant wife to become a catholic as well.[31] When Sinn Féin and nationalist party leaders met to agree a distribution of Ulster seats among them in 1918, in order to avoid a split vote, they did so under the auspices of Cardinal Logue, catholic archbishop of Armagh, who assigned the seats as he saw fit.[32]

Among unionists the religious link was also vital. The 1885 general election involved an electoral conflict in Ulster between liberals, drawing much of their support from the presbyterians, and conservatives, drawing much of their backing from members of the Church of Ireland. In the event the conservatives defeated the liberals, partly owing to the successful integration of the Orange Order into conservative party organisation at constituency level.[33] The Orange Order was still a minority movement among protestants but it did reach out to a sizeable section of the protestant working-class electorate. In 1886 conservatives and pro-union liberals joined together to form a new unionist movement in which, thanks to their 1885 victory, the conservatives and their Orange allies were dominant. The new unionist movement was successful, but only among the protestant electorate. Neither the Orange Order nor the catholic clergy should be seen in the conspiratorial guise in which their opponents often viewed them, but should be regarded as providing important leadership and organisation for their respective groups.

In spite of the Russellite movement of the early 1900s and the presence of some catholic unionists, such as Denis Henry, M.P. for South Londonderry 1916-21, unionist politics in early twentieth-century Ulster continued to show this religious link. In 1905 the Orange Order was allocated a sizeable number of places in the new Ulster Unionist Council. The Ne Temere decree of 1907 caused great concern to Ulster unionists,[34] and for many the religious issue remained of paramount importance. Protestant clergy played a very public part in the signing of the Ulster solemn league and covenant on Saturday 28 September 1912. In his memoirs published in 1921, J.A. Rentoul, unionist M.P. for East Down, 1890-1902, was highly critical of the backing of the churches for Sir Edward Carson and the unionist party in 1912:

So widespread was the clerical support accorded by the various protestant denominations to his party, that a brotherhood, hitherto undreamt of among these sects, became the order of the day.

Not only did protestant primates and bishops, presbyterian moderators and ex-moderators, Methodist presidents and vice-presidents, vie with each other in their eagerness to rally round his standard, but there took place what might almost be described as a miracle of grace, for a minister of the presbyterian church (Rev. Dr Irwin, moderator of the assembly) was permitted – for, I believe, the first time ... to preach from an episcopal pulpit, that of Belfast cathedral.

Anniversary services of thanksgiving for covenant day became common in many churches. Church premises were available for recording the signatures of those approving of the new movement, and the protestant clergy who stood aloof from these things were regarded almost as traitors to their faith.[35]

On the Monday following the signing of the Ulster Covenant, the *Northern Whig* declared: 'Home rule is at bottom a war against protestantism, an attempt to establish a Roman Catholic ascendancy in this country ...'.[36]

The two new states in Ireland post 1921 reflected strongly these links between religion and politics. In the north the

new state became identified closely with the protestant community. The unionist party which remained in power from
1921 to 1972 was almost exclusively protestant and efforts in
the late 1950s and 1960s to widen its confessional base were
rejected, in particular by the leadership of the Orange Order
in 1959. All Northern Ireland prime ministers and most
unionist M.P.s were members of the Orange Order. In the
field of educational matters, protestant church interests
obtained a settlement in 1929 which was favourable to protestant needs in the new state system. On matters such as Sunday
observance the protestant ethos prevailed. Speaking in 1932,
Lord Craigavon declared that 'ours is a protestant government and I am an Orangeman' while two years later he stated
that : 'in the south they boasted of a catholic state ... All I
boast of is that we are a protestant parliament and a protestant state.'[37] Similarly, the nationalist party in Northern
Ireland remained closely identified with the catholic community. Catholic clergy continued to be important in nationalist politics until the 1960s.[38]

   In the last twenty-five years the connection between religion and politics in Northern Ireland has been questioned,
not least by prominent members of the churches themselves.
A report of the church and government committee of the
presbyterian church in Ireland delivered at a special assembly
at Coleraine in September 1990 spoke of the need to 'distance ourselves from the kind of protestantism which closely
identifies the reformed faith with particular political and cultural aspirations.'[39] The link between the Orange Order and
the unionist party has been questioned in recent years from
within both the Order and the unionist party. Cardinal Cahal
Daly has challenged the assumptions of many, both protestant and catholic, by drawing a distinction between his personal political views and his pronouncements as a bishop,
and by seeking to distance the catholic church from nationalism.[40]

   In the period after 1921 there were also strong links in the
south between religion and politics, which had an important
bearing on north/south relations. Direct catholic clerical
involvement in politics declined rapidly in the 1920s and

1930s as the nationalist political movement divided in a number of directions.[41] But Irish politicians maintained close links with church leaders, and the catholic ethos was central to the new state. J.H. Whyte, in his important study of church-state relations in twentieth century Ireland, rejected the view that Ireland was a theocratic state but he acknowledged that the catholic church had a strong hold on the loyalty of the people and that the catholic moral code became enshrined in the legislation of the new state.[42] In areas of education, health and social welfare the catholic church played a key role. Rarely, except in a few cases such as the mother and child scheme of 1951, did the tranquil relations of church and state break down. Politicians were often effusive in their acknowledgement of the special place of the catholic church in Ireland. An address to Pope Pius XI in 1925, presented by W.T. Cosgrave, began with the words: 'Humbly prostrate at the feet of your holiness, we, your Irish children, offer our loyal devotion and deep affection. We come from a land which has ever been faithful to the See of Rome.'[43] When Dublin corporation passed a resolution tendering devotion to the pope in the 1950 holy year, Robert Briscoe, T.D., a Jewish member of the corporation, declared that Ireland was a catholic country and the more catholic the people became, the more he liked it.[44]

Recent decades have seen a weakening in relations between the catholic church and the state in the south. In 1972 the catholic bishops accepted without demur the removal of the reference to the 'special position' of the catholic church from the Irish constitution. In his book on relations between the Vatican and Irish governments, Professor Dermot Keogh draws attention to a speech in 1985 by Mr Peter Barry, the republic's foreign minister, which marked a new stage in church state relations.[45] Mr Barry stated: 'It cannot seriously be denied that during the fifty years which followed the establishment of an independent Irish state, there was a considerable intimacy between the state and the catholic church.' He acknowledged the contribution of the catholic church in areas such as education but he recorded the concern that 'the alliance of church and

state was harmful for both parties.' He believed that
relations between the two had changed considerably since
1972 to a point when, during the deliberations of the
New Ireland Forum in 1984, the catholic church leaders
publicly accepted that all churches had an equal right to
speak out on public affairs and that parliament had the
right to legislate as it saw fit. This speech by a leading
government minister, Keogh believes, served as a
significant rebuff to the catholic church and represented
a key stage in the evolution of a pluralist society in the
republic.

In both the Republic of Ireland and Northern Ireland
the role of the churches in the politics of their respective
states has also been weakened by other factors. In the
south the catholic church faces a growing liberalisation and
pluralism, while at the same time the numbers of clergy
and religious sisters are dropping due to lack of vocations.
As a reflection of new attitudes, we may note the lack
of open criticism from church sources to the latest government proposals to limit church influence in school boards
in the south. Recent scandals, such as those concerning
Father Brendan Smyth and Bishop Eamon Casey, have
damaged church authority. Protestant churches in the
north also face a diminution of their role in society. The
influence of protestant church representatives on school
boards has been challenged. A recent survey noted the
drop in church attendance among many, especially the
young.[46] Growing liberalisation in the north has undermined some traditional protestant values, such as Sunday
closing.

On a positive note we may observe the growth in friendly
relations between many on both sides of the religious
divide, at both clerical and lay levels. Organisations such
as the Irish School of Ecumenics and Corrymeela have
played an important role in this respect. While acknowledging the misunderstandings and differences between
the churches, the church and government committee
of the presbyterian church in its report of 1993 declared:

Despite the continuing and in some ways increasing fear and suspicion between the 'two communities' in the north, there has
been an encouraging growth in relationships, communication
and understanding between the main protestant churches and
the Roman catholic church, compared with the situation prior to
the Vatican council and before the present era of the Troubles
began. Joint statements by church leaders, joint reports through
interchurch bodies and pronouncements and appeals by the
churches severally have displayed a considerable degree of una-
nimity. There has been concerted condemnation of violence and
a consistent plea for political dialogue.[47]

Some special political aspects of the religious dimension
are worth mentioning. First, Professor Pádraig O'Malley
has argued that religion is important because it
gives protestants and catholics a different approach to
language.[48] Because of their strong biblical approach
to religion, protestants are literalists while catholics are
not. Both the Anglo-Irish Agreement and the Downing
Street Declaration caused problems for protestants
because they found the language vague or because they
took exception to particular clauses. For catholics,
however, these statements only provided broad principles
and their vagueness was seen as creating useful latitude
for discussion. Secondly, Cardinal Cahal Daly has spoken
on how religious ideas have become secularised and
misused by paramilitaries:

In the republican tradition, themes of blood sacrifice, resurrec-
tion and the burial rituals for dead volunteers, take on a quasi-
sacred significance and become a secularised form of
catholicism. This has been studied in respect of some of the writings of Padraig Pearse. In the loyalist tradition, slogans such as
'for God and Ulster,' the symbolism of the open bible placed
upon the Ulster flag, sometimes accompanied by a rifle or
crossed rifles, illustrate on one hand the secularisation of protestantism into loyalist politics, and on the other hand the sacralis-
ing of loyalist political themes.[49]

IV

In conclusion, then, it may be argued that religion has indeed been a real factor in the politics of Northern Ireland as it has in many other countries in Western Europe. From the view point of an historian or a political scientist, religion serves as an ideology which influences and binds whole communities. This point was acknowledged by Dr Robin Eames, Church of Ireland Archbishop of Armagh, in an interview in 1992 when he sought to explain how and why religion is important. He stated: 'Where the difficulties have arisen is where Christianity has become "religion" and that religion in turn has become ideology. It has become a thing of cultures, traditions and generations.'[50] Looking at the experience of many other countries in Western Europe, where there has been either a protestant/catholic balance or a catholic majority with important political consequences, it is very unlikely that Northern Ireland or the Republic of Ireland could have escaped this problem. Those who blame British imperialism or capitalism for the conflict in Northern Ireland must realise that in very different circumstances in Western Europe religion has remained an integral variable in the politics of many countries. Given the depth of religious feeling and division in Ireland, it is hard to see how religion could not have been an important factor in our politics.

Undoubtedly, individuals, groups and interests have used the religious division to their advantage. Conversely, it is also true that church leaders have used the political situation to their advantage. The problem in Northern Ireland does involve other issues such as conflicts over nationality, over power or over territory but the religious element remains a basic one which affects all the others. Without the religious division, nationalism or unionism in Northern Ireland would be subject to the normal rise or fall of electoral support due to party competition: the fixed, confessional nature of nationalism and unionism make this impossible. The European dimensions must be continually stressed. Historically and in the present century our community shares that common European experience of dealing with the effect of religion and its divisions in the political arena. Elsewhere in the world today, whether in America with the growth of the Christian right movement or in countries in the Middle East and Africa with the rise of Islam as a political force, religion remains a significant force in politics. The situation in Northern Ireland is, therefore, unfortunately not unique.

At the same time as acknowledging the key role of religion we have also noted two very important qualifications. One of these is that in other countries people have found ways of accommodating these differences. This does not mean that the divisions can be forgotten easily. Even in Holland confessional parties remained extremely influential until the 1970s, and in various catholic countries Christian Democratic parties have retained their church links. But these countries have found ways to cope with the differences and to reach accommodation across such divisions. Clearly it should be possible for us to do the same. The second point is that any division, whether arising from religion or any other issue, is strongly affected by its relations with other divisions. In our case the link between religion and nationalism, as expressed by unionist or nationalist, is very important. Decoupling these forces will clearly affect each of them.

When we consider the future it is difficult to forecast how important religion and religious division will continue to be for the politics of our community. It has been argued that the changes in the influence of the churches, north and south, will have only minimal effect for the Northern Ireland conflict, partly because people are so deeply immersed in these sectarian patterns of thought and action that they will not change easily, and partly because important groups in the churches are still capable of influential political intervention.[51] Such arguments warn us not to expect rapid change. At the same time, it is clear that many people today in the political parties and in the churches challenge this state of affairs. The link between the protestant and catholic sides and the respective forces of unionism and nationalism is now being questioned as damaging to both religion and the political parties. Politicians increasingly realise the limits imposed on their parties' potential support by these sectarian limitations. Church people are increasingly aware of the damage done to the Christian message by their political connections. Such developments may help to promote further change in this critical area of religion and politics in our society.

4

THE USE AND ABUSE OF HISTORY
IN IRELAND TODAY

In the language and world view of politicians there are frequent references to the past or to history in Ireland. In his speech to the annual conference of the Democratic Unionist Party in November 1995, Rev. Ian Paisley declared that 'the spirit which inspired our forefathers to refuse to bow the knee to the enemies of liberty still burns in the breasts of their sons and daughters.'[1] He then attacked the government for their handling of the controversy over an Orange parade in the summer at Drumcree, near Portadown: 'At the Somme it was rightly said that the men of Ulster were lions but the English officers directing the battle were asses.' In his oration at Wolfe Tone's grave at Bodenstown, Co. Kildare, in June 1992, leading Sinn Fein spokesman Jim Gibney stated that republicans are governed 'not by the tantrums of the season, not by the daily chore of a nine to five job:' he continued: 'Blood flows in their veins surely, but their hearts beat to the sound of a distant drum calling them to an ancient and noble cause.'[2] When Ruaire Ó Brádaigh of Republican Sinn Féin was asked about the international influences on Irish nationalism he stated: 'In Ireland we have no need of your Che Guevaras and your Ho Chi Minhs. We have Robert Emmet, O'Donovan Rossa, Cathal Brugha, Dan Breen.'[3]

In other areas also, references to the past are made frequently. At the beginning of her recent novel, *House of*

splendid isolation, set in the west of Ireland, Edna O'Brien
declares: 'History is everywhere. It seeps into the soil, the sub-
soil. Like rain, or hail, or snow, or blood. A house remembers.
An outhouse remembers. A people ruminate. The tale differs
with the teller'.[4] In his book, *Trinity*, Leon Uris concludes
with the words: 'In Ireland, there is no future, only the past
happening over and over'.[5] The past is used often to explain
or excuse the state of a wide range of matters in Ireland, from
the poor state of the economy, to various social ills and even
to the destruction of the architectural heritage. Dermot
Bolger, the novelist, has complained that 'we must go back
three centuries to explain any fight outside a chip shop'.[6]

I

This constant reference to the past deserves special attention.
Ireland, north and south, like all countries, is influenced by
its history. In our case, however, we seem to use the past as an
explanation for the present more often than most other
places. Of course, it could be argued that this is because we
have 'unresolved' historical problems, which are part of a
special deterministic history going back, in many unionists'
views, to the seventeenth century, or, in many nationalists'
views, to the twelfth century. Such an argument could be used
easily to explain the situation in other places, but rarely is.
For example, the problem of class conflict in England today
could be seen as part of an unending conflict going back to
the Peasants' Revolt of the fourteenth century or the civil war
of the seventeenth century, but few would care to take this
view. Events of the remote past cannot be ignored in either
England or Ireland, but the main features of our present-day
society, in Ireland as in other European countries, owe much
more to the recent developments of the late nineteenth and
twentieth centuries when, in our case, conflict over nationalism and religious division emerged as crucial. Events of the
remote past are just as important, or as unimportant, for our
society as for any other.

Nonetheless, many observers have remarked that people
in Ireland are 'obsessed' with the past. Dr A.T.Q. Stewart has
commented: 'To the Irish all history is applied history and

the past is simply a convenient quarry which provides ammunition to use against enemies in the present'.[7] The use of history in this manner is not a new phenomenon, as a number of historians have pointed out.[8] Then as now, our concern about the past is strongly influenced by our present preoccupations. Our real interest in and concern for history is actually quite limited. Speaking at the Merriman summer school in 1993, Professor Joe Lee of Cork pointed out that 'less than a quarter of leaving certificate students took history, a smaller proportion than the norm elsewhere. The amount of research into Irish history being carried out at Irish educational institutions was at an extraordinary low level'.[9] In Northern Ireland the situation is little better.

In an address to the 1989 conference of the Cultural Traditions Group, Mr Jack Magee concluded that 'The Irish, despite what outsiders believe, are not preoccupied with history but obsessed with divisive and largely sectarian mythologies acquired as part of their political or religious experience.'[10] In an incisive paper written nearly two decades earlier, he had pointed out how much of our knowledge of the past is picked up from popular legends and songs, often in the home.[11] Elsewhere in this book we have examined in greater detail how people selectively view the past, and how myths or half-truths about our history develop. Our concern about the past is strongly influenced by our present preoccupations and outlooks, which colour the sense of history which we develop. For example, nationalists will remember the Easter Rising of 1916 but forget those Irish nationalists who died in France in the British army in the same year, while unionists will recall the Battle of the Boyne and yet ignore the Battle of Ballynahinch when many protestants fought as United Irishmen. The present influences our views of the past. The other aspect to this matter, however, is the interesting issue of how these views of the past can influence our actions today. The past is no more important here than elsewhere but people believe that it is, and that gives it a special role. Views of the past, often mythical ones, are an important dynamic in modern Ireland, north and south.

From an examination of contemporary comment, in newspapers and elsewhere, it is clear that the past and the myths
of the past, are used in a number of ways for various purposes,
both in Northern Ireland and in the Republic of Ireland, with
important consequences. As regards the impact of myths in
Ireland the author, Eugene McCabe, has commented
recently:

> throughout the country, family mythology, local mythology, his-
> torical mythology, should all be tagged with a health warning:
> 'Myth can induce a form of madness and zealotry that leads to
> death.[12]

People often employ history as a reason for actions or inac-
tions. The excuse of history can be used to diminish a sense
of responsibility and initiative from the individual. Citizens
sometimes respond to current problems, not in an effective
way, but in a manner that can be damaging because it is based
on historical myths and not on a realistic view of the current
situation. History can be used to supply role models or simple answers. History can provide grievances for contemporary use, it can give an influential deterministic view of things
and it can create traditions which weigh heavily on current
events. In a situation of intercommunal conflict as in Ireland,
arguments over history often create a dead locked situation
as one side can always counter the other side's historical
grievances with grievances of their own. This phenomenon ,
of course, is found in many countries. Most societies use the
past and myths about the past to a certain extent,[13] but some,
including Ireland, seem to do so more than others. Quebec
and South Africa are two such states where historical arguments have been an important part of modern political
debate.[14] In the case of South Africa, history was used to
justify apartheid[15], while in recent years there has been a
conscious effort to avoid this type of argument.[16]

II

Turning again to Ireland, let us look first at the Republic of
Ireland. In 1966 the Taoiseach Séan Lemass commented:

Our hopes in the future rest on our confidence in ourselves and
on the final dying out of the old slave spirit which, in the past,
bedevilled our efforts to get the nation reorganised for progress,
and which still influences the behaviour of some individuals. In
the next half century we will no longer be able to find in history
an excuse for our failure in any field of activity, if we should fail.[17]

The evidence, however, shows that his words have been little
heeded. If we study comments by current commentators and
politicians, we can find plentiful examples of the past being
used to account for or to explain away many present-day
problems.

A classic example of this use of history occurred in a report
on Co. Laois in the *Irish Times* on 17 June 1991 by Renagh
Holohan. She described an introverted and fractious people
who lacked self-esteem, motivation and leadership. This state
of affairs was attributed to the traumatic effects of the plantation of the county in the sixteenth century. The county, it was
further stated, had 'few, if any, famous sons or daughters'. On
6 July 1991 Charles Flanagan, T.D., wrote to the paper to
protest strongly about the article and the way that history was
being used. He stated the current leadership which controlled the county council should do something positive and
not just complain. Flanagan also objected to the fact that the
article had ignored important people whom the county had
produced, such as Bartholomew Mosse who set up the
Rotunda Hospital in Dublin, Thomas Prior who founded the
Royal Dublin Society and Lucy Franks, foundress of the Irish
Countrywomen's Association. Of course, Holohan and those
to whom she had spoken, ignored these historic figures mentioned by Flanagan because most were Anglo-Irish and were
therefore regarded as unsuitable for inclusion in such a survey of the county and its past.

One aspect of the danger of this selective use of history has
been referred to by President Mary Robinson. In an address
to the Cultures of Ireland group at Dun Laoghaire in
September 1991, she mentioned a recent visit to Birr to look
at the great telescope of the third Earl of Rosse and recalled
other notable Irish scientists such as Robert Boyle (1627–91).

But in twentieth-century Irish culture, she complained, these people have been ignored because they are seen as Anglo-Irish and not part of the Irish nation, with the result that there is a poor sense of a scientific tradition in much of Ireland.[18] In fact Ireland has a valuable scientific tradition, but this has been ignored because of such attitudes. She called for a inclusive view of Irish history.

In the *Sunday Tribune* on 20 June 1993, in an otherwise valuable and interesting survey of the Irish economy, Paul Tansey commented: 'In the race to catch up with Europe, Ireland has been impeded by both historical and geographic barriers. History handicapped Ireland making it a latecomer to economic development'. Yet Professor Joe Lee has shown that in 1910, on the eve of independence, Ireland's level of gross national product *per capita* was above that of Norway, Sweden, Italy and Finland. By 1970, however, after a record of the slowest growth of *per capita* income of any European country except the UK, every country beneath Ireland in 1910 had closed the gap or overtaken Ireland.[19] In 1921 the new state had no national debt but in the last decade its debt has been one of the highest in the world. Other countries, such as Korea and Taiwan, which started less than 50 years ago with a considerable 'historical handicap' have long since surpassed Ireland in economic development. The blame for Ireland's poor economic position in the twentieth century is not to do with history but with the failure of modern Irish political and economic policies.

In many other areas the past is used to explain away or to excuse problems. The novelist, Dermot Bolger, has written of how writers 'are presumed to view the world through somebody else's obsessive relationship with England and to be so bizarrely entangled with history that we must go back three centuries to explain any fight outside a chip shop'.[20] He refers here to a strong emphasis in the literary/academic world to see matters greatly influenced by a 'colonial' and then 'post colonial' view of Irish history. This approach to the Irish past started in the 1960s and has become in vogue owing to its ability to satisfy both the traditional nationalist perspective and modern literary theory.[21] Most historians would be reluctant to see Irish history in a simple colonial model, although they accept aspects of colonisation in periods of Irish history. But others, especially in the *Field Day anthology* and associated pamphlets, see it as essential to account for all sorts of Irish failings.

A narrow view of the past has had a harmful effect on the architectural heritage of Ireland. In his book, *The destruction of Dublin*, Frank McDonald has described how the demolition of many of Dublin's Georgian buildings began in the late 1950s with the knocking down of some impressive houses in Kildare Place by the Office of Public Works: 'Echoing a view quite common at the time among narrow-minded nationalists that Georgian architecture was part of the legacy of '800 years of oppression,' one government minister actually said, 'I was glad to see them go. They stood for everything I hate.'[22] Since that time many other fine buildings have been destroyed, in part due to the survival of such attitudes. Recently, however, there has been something of a change of opinion. Fianna Fáil has now produced a policy document on urban renewal which urges that Georgian houses in central Dublin should be restored to their former use as family dwellings which will 'ensure that our heritage will be preserved for generations to come.'[23] Speaking at a conference on the future of the country house in Ireland in February 1993, the Taoiseach Mr Albert Reynolds declared:

> The destruction of the likes of Coole Park and Bowen's Court and latent hostility or bureaucratic and commercial indifference is tending to give way more to a growing realisation and sense of pride that the many splendid monuments of the past such as Dublin Castle and the Royal Hospital, Kilmainham are jewels that now belong to an independent, democratic Irish nation, and we need have no complexes about their origins.[24]

Although he used the word 'tending' this statement represented a considerable change in official attitudes to the past in the matter of the architectural heritage.

Elsewhere we can find frequent references to the past in current terminology. In an editorial on the Taoiseach's decision to hold a referendum before settling the abortion question in 1992, the *Nationalist and Leinster Times* used graphic historical allusions:

> Over the centuries, [the people's] forefathers resisted foreign efforts to impose alien politics and religion. The Irish did not sell their souls for a mess of pottage then, no matter how big the mess seemed to have been ... Is the present Reynold's government of the opinion that the present generation will sell out where their forefathers didn't and that ministers can succeed with promises, bribes and threats where the dungeon, fire and sword failed.[25]

In the same year journalists in R.T.E. were criticised for avoiding using the terms 'murder' or 'terrorist' in reporting on events in Northern Ireland. Mr Joe Mulholland, Head of News at R.T.E., responded: 'we have generally avoided using the word 'terrorist' because we feel that using it goes against the historical traditions in this country.'[26] On the seventieth anniversary of the Garda Síochána in 1992, the minister for Justice, Mr Pádraig Flynn, stated:

> This year we celebrate an important chapter in Irish history - after long struggle, we came to nationhood. In the twenties, thirties and forties, great challenges were faced by our fledgling democracy. Huge demands on their loyalty and devotion were placed on all the servants of the state in those early years. Especially so in 1922, when the Irish people, who for 700 years knew only authority backed up by brute force, were suddenly asked to submit to civil authority vested in a small number of unarmed men in blue uniforms.[27]

In an article on the subject of the Great Famine in 1994, Mr John Waters of the *Irish Times* wrote of '800 years of slavery' and attributed to the Famine many problems in Ireland today from alcoholism and schizophrenia to emigration: this drew a wide range of letters to the editor including a number which pointed out that other countries, without this historical experience, also suffer from these problems.[28]

This sense of history has affected mainstream politics and Anglo-Irish relations. Mr Desmond O'Malley, T.D., has recalled the personnel and atmosphere of the Dáil when he entered it in 1968:

> The Dáil still had figures who had played a prominent part in the war of independence and in the civil war. For some of them, the civil war had never really ended. Their conversation was often backward-looking and historical events excited them more than current events.[29]

Such veterans have now almost all gone from the political scene, but references to the past still occur. In her recent memoirs, Mrs Margaret Thatcher recalled a meeting with Dr Garret FitzGerald when he talked of 'eight hundred years of misunderstandings'.[30] Likewise when Mr Albert Reynolds first met the British prime minister Mr John Major he took him back to the 'historic basics of the Irish question'.[31] After a meeting between a unionist delegation with members of the Irish government in November 1992 Mr Ken Maginnis remarked:

> The real disappointment was that the Fianna Fáil party was caught by a large 1922 time-warp. You only had to look at some of their papers ... to see that sort of language. There was no reality in terms of 1992 – there was no attempt to understand the unionist position.[32]

In the U.S.A. in March 1993 Mr Reynolds declared on the Larry King radio show that 'history has created a border in Ireland which has outlived its usefulness', and he added that the creative potential of the people of Ireland could only be realised when ' this last residual problem in Anglo-Irish relations derived from history is finally and peacefully resolved'.[33]

During 1993, however, it is possible to observe the beginning of a slightly different approach to the past. On 3 April 1993, at the annual conference of the labour party in Waterford, Mr Dick Spring declared: 'Let us be prepared to cast off the chains of history, to stop being prisoners of our upbringing'.[34] Two weeks later, in response to questions about changes to articles two and three of the Irish constitution, Mr Reynolds stated: 'We are not tied up in our past. We want to move forward, to look at the changes required to ensure that both communities can live together'.[35] On 18 June and 7 October, Mr Spring spoke of the need to shake off the 'baggage of history'.[36] On the latter occasion his remarks evoked scepticism from Bruce Arnold in the *Irish Independent*, 9 October 1993:

> No one in this country is in favour of shaking off the baggage of history. We hug it round constantly, and it is difficult to identify which segment of political expression is most burdened. Among leading contender for the prize there are three groupings: Fianna Fáil, the unionists and Sinn Fein. Better to settle for the old enlightenments and accept that they will change, at best, inch by bloody inch, both now and in the future.

In his address to the Fianna Fáil Ard-Fheis on 6 November 1993, however, Mr Reynolds acknowledged that there was ' a more complex situation than existed during the independence struggle from 1916 to 1921', and stated that 'we must not be prisoners of history' and that 'new patterns of co-operation must transcend the antagonisms of a century between the two political cultures'.[37] Five weeks later, the Downing Street Joint Declaration was published. It spoke of the need 'to remove the causes of conflict, to overcome the legacy of history and to heal the divisions which have resulted'.[38] In a perceptive article a few days later in the *Sunday Independent*, Eamon Dunphy praised the declaration for its embodiment of the efforts of John Major and Albert Reynolds to deal firmly with present situation: 'without any reference to the past, they have identified the apparently mundane realities of the present'. He continued: 'Reynolds and Major have redefined heroism as compromise, insisted that the deal is more important than the cause, that the future matters more than the past and is accessible to all who will admit that they were wrong'.[39]

How far all this represents a real change in attitudes to the past remains to be seen. Southern leaders are certainly viewing the past differently from their approach in the early 1990s. On the Gerry Kelly U.T.V. programme, 3 March 1995, Mr

Reynolds urged people not to live in the past. His final words, however, called for everyone to look back to 1920 and the government of Ireland act with its proposed council of Ireland. He recalled King George V's speech at the opening of the Northern Ireland parliament when he urged toleration and expressed a wish that both sides should work together. This shows an effort to interpret the past in a new and more positive way. Of course it avoids the historical facts that it was the south and not the north who failed to make the council work, and that King George's urging of people to come together envisaged this as happening under the British crown.

III

Attention must now be turned to the situation in Northern Ireland. In general matters, the past seems to be referred to less in the north than in the south of Ireland. In political affairs, however, we can find very many instances of the past being used for various purposes, such as the provision of role models, of historic grievances for contemporary consumption or of deterministic views of events which can influence affairs of the present. The influence of the past is especially strong with the paramilitaries. In his book, *The Irish troubles: a generation of violence, 1967-92*, published in 1993, J. Bowyer Bell commented on how the paramilitaries, Orange and Green, have used the past:

> Those who sought to act on events, to make history to history's patterns, had the legitimisation of the past as authority. They needed only to rationalise on occasion, kill to the sound of trumpets. Elsewhere others were emboldened by Lenin's or Mao's example, by Allah's word or the people's need. The enemy was killed by the book. But in Ireland he was killed to history's tune and the blare of those unseen trumpets, audible always to the faithful. In Ireland legitimacy was won from history, a legacy and clearly defined responsibility.[40]

In his study of their many periodicals and journals over the period 1966–92, Professor Richard Davis has surveyed 'the attitude of republicans and loyalists to a history which both acknowledge as fundamental to their respective positions.'[41]

In the case of the provisional I.R.A. there is plenty of evidence of the impact of the past. A former I.R.A. volunteer, Shane O'Doherty, has described his reasons for joining the I.R.A.:

> My attraction to the I.R.A. was not initially based on the sight or experience of any particular social injustice, though, when I did join the I.R.A., injustices were foremost in my motivation. It was the discovery of the tragedies of Irish history which first caused my desire to give myself to the I.R.A., and the best part of that history I imbibed alone at home reading books I found in the family library. It was the pure political injustice and tragedy of British rule in Ireland against the wishes of the Irish people which fired my anger, not forgetting the Famine and mass emigration.[42]

He recalls reading the writings of the executed leaders of 1916, and of earlier patriots: 'these writings ignited in me a passionate patriotism and an equally passionate desire to emulate the heroic deeds recounted therein.' Republican magazines such as *Iris* and *An Phoblacht* contain many historical articles on subjects such as the 1916 rising and Irish political martyrs. *An Phoblacht*, 30 April 1972, declared that, 'The modern Sinn Féin of 1972 is the same organisation as was founded in 1905 and has the same objectives as it set itself in 1918' while on 15 April 1982 the paper stated that, 'we are confident that the I.R.A. stands ready and able, as the I.R.A. did in 1916.'

Observers have commented on this republican use of history. Pádraig O'Malley has pointed out how in 1981 the hunger-strikers in their last days listened to extracts from *Trinity*, Leon Uris' fictional account of the 1916 rising.[43] O'Malley characterised the I.R.A. as caught in its own traditions. Others have made the same point. Cardinal Cahal Daly spoke in Christmas1992 of the I.R.A. being caught in a 'time warp' while Séamus Mallon in 1993 remarked how they were 'weighed down by history'.[44] After a particularly brutal murder by the I.R.A. in 1992 in South Armagh of a person who had allegedly been an informer, Dundalk priest Fr John Duffy reacted angrily: 'I could not believe that someone could be dumped on the roadside, naked, hooded and mutilated. If this is how you write Irish history then it is not worth giving it to anyone'.[45] The journalist Dick Walsh wrote in December 1993 that I.R.A. members 'see themselves as a force apart, responding only to the commands of history'.[46] A South African journalist, Rian Malan, in the same year remarked that the I.R.A. members were 'so steeped in ancestral memories of martyrdom that they can't see straight anymore'.[47]

For loyalist paramilitaries the past is also very important. In the *Church of Ireland Gazette* in January 1995 the commentator 'Cromlyn' described how they seek the sanction of history:

> loyalist paramilitarism, [sees] itself in this generation as guardian of an inherited sacred trust, linked in direct succession to those of their forefathers who over and over again have barricaded themselves into their chosen territory and shouted defiance from where they stood with an ancestral gun in their hands.[48]

If we turn to magazines such as *Combat* or *New Ulster Defender*, we can read articles about the Somme and the original U.V.F.. These papers also carry articles about ancient Ulster, especially the deeds of the Cruthin. Cuchulainn, the ancient Celtic hero, has been claimed as a loyalist hero. A wall mural erected in East Belfast in 1994 shows Cuchulainn linked in support with a 'B' Special and a member of the U.D.R. Standish O'Grady in the late nineteenth century was responsible for developing the heroic tale of Cuchulainn who was later taken up by republicans as a hero against the English invader and is the subject of a statue in the Dublin G.P.O. commemorating the 1916 rising.[49] Loyalists have now adopted him as an Ulster hero who kept enemies from the rest of Ireland out of Ulster.

Among politicians of our constitutional parties there are frequent references to the past. We can see this in the speeches of M.P.s in the debate on the Anglo-Irish Agreement in parliament in 1985.[50] Mr John Hume talked of events of 1912, stated that 'the divisions in Ireland go back well beyond partition' and referred to the United Irishmen and C.S. Parnell. Rev. Ian Paisley declared:

> Anyone who has read history should understand that this did not start in 1920, but goes far back to the days of the plantation settlement and back into the dim and distant past. There have been continued efforts to destroy the British presence in Ireland.

Mr Peter Robinson read from Rudyard Kipling's 'Ulster 1912' and quoted Wilfrid Spender on Ulster bravery and sacrifices at the Somme, while Mr Harold McCusker reminded his listeners how the Irish Free State had reneged on its agreement of 1925 concerning the status of Northern Ireland.

Turning specifically to unionists, we can observe how history influences their actions. Orange parades remind unionists annually of the sacrifices and bravery of their seventeenth century ancestors (see chapter 1). Unionists often talk of the 'age old enemy' or the 'traditional enemy'. In mid-1993 Rev. Ian Paisley warned of the danger of the people of the province being sold 'like cattle on the hoof to their traditional enemies', while in early 1995 he described how unionists faced a threat engineered by 'the vicious aggression of their traditional enemies'.[51] Professor Steve Bruce has commented on the unionist use of the past.

> Things were once very good when all of Ireland was British. Then they were good because Ulster was British. Any future is hardly likely to be better than the past and is almost certain to be worse. The most successful unionist politicians are those whose manner and style, as well as politics, are most obviously tied to the past. Even when it is presented as the last chance to hold on to the present, innovation is suspect because it is an admission that something must be given up.[52]

Dr Alvin Jackson has described how unionist politicians, in particular Rev. Ian Paisley, have sought to model their actions on those of Craig and Carson in 1912. Writing in 1990, Dr Jackson commented on unionist opposition to the Anglo-Irish Agreement:

Both Democratic and Official Unionists have agreed in seeing their resistance to the Anglo-Irish Agreement as a reconstruction of their forefathers' opposition to the third home rule bill – even if they differ over the inheritance of individual roles. The immutability of their dilemma has impressed all types of unionist. As with Frank McGuinness's Kenneth Pyper, ancestral hands exercise a guidance and constraint from beyond the grave. A particular sense of history and a particular cast of mind permit the present to be fulfilled by the events of a long-dead struggle.[53]

Concern about the past can also be found on the nationalist side. At the end of 1992, the *Irish News* warned of the danger of misuse of the past.

There is much to be said for looking forward rather than back. Little is gained by dwelling on the past, the people of Ireland know that perhaps more than any other nation. Indeed many of the troubles which beset Ireland at this end of the 20th century have been caused by those who believe it is more important to build a country fit for our ancestors rather than our children.

It has become popular to blame history for our present situation. But the real blame lies with the tunnel vision of those who prefer to take a partial view of the history of this island.

These people are in a tiny minority, yet by exploiting the fears of others they have gained the initiative. Slowly but surely the paramilitaries are bringing us to our knees. They have successfully blocked political progress and they have been able to elude the security forces.[54]

In spite of this criticism of the misuse of history, however, the *Irish News* itself dwells much on the past. It sometimes prints historical articles of an old-fashioned fundamentalist nationalist type. For example, an article in summer 1992 on the Co. Cork, gentry, background of Sir Patrick Mayhew, described how the landlords had frequently indulged in the rape of women on their estates.[55] Just as so many black people have white men's blood, because of masters raping their slaves, so in Ireland many people had landlord blood, according to the writer. This hysterical and untrue article led to one correspondent complaining to the paper of the writer's promotion of 'fantasy masquerading as political or historical analysis' and of the use of family anecdote to 'perpetuate myth and prejudice'. Everyday the *Irish News* carries a column, usually underneath its editorial column recalling events in the years 1912-14 or 1920-3. Frequently it deals with injustices perpetrated on the nationalist and catholic people of the province. Such events actually occurred but so did other things such as wrongs done to protestants and unionists, and so did other matters of national or international importance, but these are rarely recalled.

During 1993 we can see evidence of the beginning of a movement away from the past. In an interview in early October 1993 Mr Gerry Adams responded to a question about change in the republican movement: 'we have adopted a different approach which is more in keeping with the reality of Ireland in 1993 than perhaps harking back to Ireland in 1918'.[56] On the popular B.B.C. programme 'Spotlight' on 21 October 1993 Mr John Hume spoke of the 'distrust of others based on the past', and urged that now was the time to leave the past. In an article in the *Observer* in September 1994, he declared:

> There is a lot in our past that all sides continually complain of. Indeed, in many ways, Northern Ireland politics have always been about the past. The time has come to draw a line over that past. Let history judge it and let us look for the first time to a future in which we can reach an agreement that respects our diversity.[57]

Nevertheless, opinions continue to differ over events such as the 1918 general election, with Sinn Féin emphasising it and John Hume saying that it only confirmed divisions.[58] At a conference on the future of Northern Ireland at the University of North London in early March 1995 David Ervine, leader of the Progressive Unionist party, appealed for nationalists and unionist to shed the 'myths' of the past and build a new future that accomodates the aspirations of both communities. He spoke of the need to 'break the myth and bury the ghosts'.[59]

As regards the paramilitaries, we can observe that the recent ceasefires have an important historical setting. In the case of the loyalist groups, it is worth noting that the ceasefire declaration of the Combined Loyalist Military Command in October 1994 was made in the Glencairn estate at Fernhill House, a building with historic links to the original U.V.F.. The report of this event in the loyalist periodical *Combat* had a headline 'Historic place, historic time'.[60] This historical gesture no doubt was meant to assure supporters that this new step was not out of line with their origins. At the same time the statement carried no references to the historical background beyond the recent troubles.

In the case of the Provisional I.R.A. their ceasefire statement at the end of August 1994 made few historical points apart from a reference to all those who had died for Irish freedom. The *Irish News* editorial, appearing on the day after the ceasefire saw their statement in the 'tradition of Patrick Pearse's noble decision to lay down arms after the Easter Rising of 1916'.[61] In the 1995 Easter edition of *An Phoblacht* the I.R.A. statement read out at republican rallies declared that 'all parties must .... resolve to leave behind the failures of the past and must .... build a new and free Ireland which removes the divisions of the past'. Noticeably, compared with the many historical articles on the 1916 Easter Rising found in previous Easter editions of *An Phoblacht*, the magazine carried little on the subject, and indeed for the first time reported critical views of the Easter Rising and its participants from writers such as Ruth Dudley Edwards.[62]

Clearly, then, the past and myths of the past are an important influence in many aspects of life in contemporary Ireland, north and south. This is especially so in matters surrounding the conflict in Northern Ireland. After President Clinton's speech to the conference on Northern Ireland in Washington in May 1995, Sir Patrick Mayhew remarked that the theme of the speech had been: 'Let us turn the key upon history and go forward into new uplands free from the bur-

dens of the history of the past.'[63] To some extent this is what
is happening. Among some politicians and spokesmen for
paramilitaries there appears to be less conscious use of the
past. How far this change is a real one it is difficult to say? In
the *Irish Times* of 20 May 1995, the journalist Dick Walsh questioned the sincerity of Sinn Féin on this matter: 'To Sinn
Féin, of course, what's happening now is the old Anglo-Irish
struggle carried on by other means. He continued 'In a direct
line with the 800 years of oppression there are two sides, the
British and the Irish; and the Irish side is represented by Sinn
Féin.' How far people in Ireland have really changed in their
use of the past is still to be seen?

There remains the interesting question of why we have
used and continue to use history in this manner. To some
extent the reason for this may be that debates and divisions
over nationalism have often used historical frameworks of
argument. To some extent also it may be that in the dominant
Anglo-American world in which we live, conflicts over nationalism and religion have not mattered significantly in recent
times in the political field and so people have emphasised
these historical arguments in order to make sense, both to
themselves and to others, of the world in which they live:
probably this reason is especially true for observers from outside Ireland. Perhaps this historical approach has become a
tradition in itself, part of our culture. Whatever the reason, it
is important not only to separate the myth from the reality of
the impact of the past, but also to ensure that this attempt to
explain constantly the present by means of myths of the past
does not in itself add significantly to the problems of the present. We face complex problems of the modern world, problems of national identify, religious division, unemployment
and inequality, and to cripple ourselves unnecessarily with
additional burdens from the past will make our difficulties all
the greater. History affects our world of the present, but we
must take care not to overestimate its impact in Ireland.
Abuse of our history threatens to influence the new contemporary history which we are forging for ourselves today.

5

COMMEMORATIONS, FESTIVALS
AND PUBLIC HOLIDAYS

'Commemoration,' President Mary Robinson has declared recently, 'is a moral act.'[1] In her 1995 Christmas message Queen Elizabeth stated: 'commemoration and anniversaries are very important elements in our national life.'[2] In Ireland, north and south, there are a number of days in the year which people celebrate because of their connection with particular historic episodes or individuals. The 17th of March and St Patrick, Easter Sunday and the Dublin Rising of 1916, the 12th of July and the Battle of the Boyne in 1690, and Remembrance Sunday when those who died in two world wars are recalled, are important annual events. In addition to these anniversaries there are special commemorations of particular episodes or persons from the past which are not annual but which take place after a certain length of time. These acts of commemoration serve to remind us of important moments in our history and for our culture. By this means we honour the achievement, bravery, endurance and suffering of earlier generations and show that we have not forgotten their efforts.

While commemoration has this moral dimension about the past, at the same time it can often serve a particular purpose in our modern world. We celebrate commemorations in the light of our needs and aspirations. Such acts of remem-

brance are often used as a symbol of unity and common interest for a community. Independence Day on 4 July and Bastille
Day on 14 July serve as powerful annual acts of national
'bonding' for the United States of America and France
respectively. In other countries, including Ireland, however,
the principal dates of remembrance are often held in high
esteem by some groups but not by others and while they may
inspire certain sections of the community, others will be dis-
interested or even offended. As Professor Edna Longley has
commented; 'Commemorations are as selective as sympa-
thies. They honour our dead, not your dead.'[3] Furthermore,
if we look at the background to these modern dates of
remembrance, we often find that the actual meaning of the
events and their 'ownership' have changed markedly over the
years. These commemorations, then, not only mark important historical occurrences or individuals, but they reflect
current attitudes, and a study of them can tell us much about
the society which commemorates the occasion and about
changes in how that society views its own history. This chapter looks at some of our principal commemorations, festivals
and national holidays and shows how their meaning has
altered over time.

I

St Patrick's Day (17 March) deserves special attention
because it has been marked so widely and for so long. At present, St Patrick's Day is celebrated in the Republic of Ireland
as a national festival. It is not only kept as a bank and state holiday, but it is the occasion of popular celebrations in many
parts of the country. In contrast, in Northern Ireland, St
Patrick's Day is marked merely as a bank holiday, and it tends
to be celebrated at the popular level primarily among the
catholic population.[4] Yet the most famous Patrician sites are
in the northern part of Ireland, and in the early years of this
century St Patrick's Day was recognised throughout Ireland
among all communities. On 18 March 1907, the Belfast
unionist newspaper, the *Northern Whig* declared in its editorial: 'Locally the recognition of St Patrick's Day is by no means
a sectional observance. All classes and creeds are at one in

their celebration of the anniversary and the shamrock was worn generally yesterday'. When President Clinton held his first St Patrick's Day celebration party at the White House in 1994, newspaper reports indicated that his Irish guests were drawn almost exclusively from the Irish catholic community in Ireland and the U.S.A.[5] The principal St Patrick's Day parade in New York is organised by officials of the Ancient Order of Hibernians. Yet the first St Patrick's Day celebrations in the American colonies were held by Irish protestants, and today protestants are a majority of the 40 million Americans who claim Irish ancestry.[6]

St Patrick, of course, is one of the most popular and most contested figures in Irish history. As Dr Charles Doherty has pointed out, 'from the late sixteenth century until very recently the debate about St Patrick has been coloured by sectarian interest.'[7] Attempts to trace their origins to Patrick have been made by many writers on church history, from James Ussher on behalf of the Church of Ireland and John Colgan on behalf of the catholic church in the early 1600s, up to rival church historians in the nineteenth and twentieth centuries. From the 1960s, owing to a growing ecumenical spirit and a determination by academics to avoid sterile debate, there has been much less effort by the leaders and historians of the main denominations to claim St Patrick exclusively as the precursor of their version of the Christian faith. Today most of the churches in Ireland would regard St Patrick as a common heritage. On St Patrick's Day 1981 Archbishop Robin Eames declared: 'St Patrick belongs to us all', while on St Patrick's Day 1988 Cardinal Tomás Ó'Fiaich stated: 'His name should be the special rallying-cry for all Christians of Irish birth or descent'.[8] Whatever the different interpretations, St Patrick has been commonly accepted as the patron saint of Ireland and from at least the seventeenth century 17 March has been observed as his feast day.

In the opening decades of the nineteenth century, as Dr Jacqueline Hill has shown in a recent study of national festivals in Ireland, in the period 1790–1829, the Irish government authorities at Dublin Castle decided to promote St Patrick's Day as a national festival.[9] The catholic popula-

tion of Ireland had long viewed St Patrick's Day as a special
day in veneration of St Patrick and on 17 March services were
commonly held in catholic churches in addition to the secular festivities. Among protestants St Patrick was well regarded
as we can see from the many Church of Ireland churches dedicated to him, and also from organisations such as the Order
of St Patrick and the Friendly Brothers of St Patrick, founded
in the eighteenth century, although in the late eighteenth
and early nineteenth centuries there seems to have been little popular celebration on St Patrick's Day among the protestant population.[10] By the last decades of the eighteenth
century St Patrick's Day was already treated by the Castle
authorities as a traditional anniversary, along with other
anniversaries such as King William's birthday. In the early
1800s, however, the government sought to move from state
symbols which were attractive to only one section of the population to those which could have broader appeal. From 1806
the government dissociated itself from the Williamite celebrations and encouraged greater support for St Patrick's Day.
In 1829 the viceroy gave St Patrick's Day special recognition
by establishing an annual ceremony of appearing at the
trooping of the colour at Dublin Castle on St Patrick's Day,
accompanied by a viceregal parade through the city and followed by a state ball in the evening.

This effort by the state in early nineteenth century Ireland
to boost St Patrick's Day as a unifying and popular symbol had
some success. The processions in Dublin became popular
with many of the citizens. On 18 March 1857 the *Freeman's
Journal* reported that; 'Yesterday being St Patrick's Day, the
now time-honoured and fully-recognised demonstration,
viceregal and popular, in honour of the anniversary of our
national saint took place'. When the lord lieutenant,
appeared on the balcony at the castle, 'an enthusiastic and
prolonged burst of applause attested the satisfaction of the
spectators'.[11] Outside Dublin the saint's day seems to have
remained primarily a day of celebration for catholics,
although there was some interest among protestants. The
Belfast Newsletter 19 March 1850 described how 'the anniversary of Ireland's patron saint was celebrated by the obser-

vance of the unusual festivities amongst our townsmen of different religious and political persuasions', including a supper organised by a local Orange lodge. Reports from the 1870s and 1880s, however, indicate that the day had taken on political and denominational overtones with the organisation of large processions, often including nationalist demonstrations.[12] A growing tendency for parades on this day to lead to violence was curtailed in the mid-1880s thanks to efforts by catholic clergy and the nationalist leadership. On the eve of St Patrick's Day 1886 C.S. Parnell issued an open letter urging restraint: 'It is at all times desirable that we should do nothing at any time to excite the irritation of the Orange section of our countrymen'.[13] In many places the catholic clergy introduced various activities such as sports and musical events to make the day more respectable and less prone to disturbance or drunkenness.

By the last decade of the nineteenth century St Patrick's Day was celebrated enthusiastically in many parts of Ireland. The *Northern Whig* in 1890 recorded how the day was marked noticeably across the province of Ulster in towns such as Newtownards, Ballymena, Derry and Newry, with their mills and factories closed: it reported that in Lisburn 'the day was ushered in by the conservative flute band'.[14] The *Freeman's Journal* in the same year described celebrations in Dublin, Cork and elsewhere in Ireland as well as overseas.[15] Outside Ireland, St Patrick's Day had become a focus for great celebration among Irish emigrants and their descendants, especially in Great Britain, the USA and Australia.[16] The anniversary was given a new boost in the late 1890s when Queen Victoria, in appreciation of the valour of Irish soldiers in the Boer War, initiated the tradition of members of the royal family presenting shamrock to Irish regiments on St Patrick's Day.

In the early 1900s, a movement began, under Gaelic League influence, to promote St Patrick's Day as Ireland's national holiday.[17] In 1903 a bill was introduced at Westminster to make St Patrick's Day a bank holiday and it quickly passed into law with no opposition - an outcome which, as the *Belfast Newsletter* commented, was 'rare good

fortune' for an Irish bill.[18] That same year the paper also
remarked: 'The anniversary helps to create a spirit of mutual
tolerance and good will amongst Irishmen and this year perhaps the spirit is more evident than before'. Throughout
Ireland in the early 1900s there were widespread celebrations
on St Patrick's Day. Besides the banks, which were closed by
law after 1903, many businesses, offices, schools and (especially) public houses were now closed on St Patrick's Day as a
result of public pressure. Church services, dinners, exhibitions, parades, sporting activities, concerts and excursions
served to inspire and entertain the population at large. From
1900 in Dublin the viceregal procession was followed later in
the day by the lord mayor's parade.

While it is clear that St Patrick's Day was celebrated in the
early 1900s more widely than at any time previously, it is also
evident that various groups valued the occasion in different
ways. In many parts, especially in the south and as a result of
the influence of the Gaelic League, the day became a focus
for Irish language enthusiasts. Perhaps because of theological
differences the saint's day was marked to a much greater
degree in catholic than protestant churches, although a few
Church of Ireland churches did use Irish in services on the
day as did many catholic churches. By 1910 the day had also
become the occasion for large political parades, particularly
those organised by the Ancient Order of Hibernians in
Ulster.[19] Among northern protestants, it is probably fair to say
that while the majority valued St Patrick's Day as a holiday
with a special Irish significance, they attached to it less of the
religious, political and cultural importance given it by others.
Nonetheless, in spite of such differences it is worth noting the
Northern Whig editorial of 18 March 1914: 'Irishmen, whatever their creed or politics have an affectionate regard for St
Patrick's Day and yesterday the shamrock was worn in honour
of the festival by fully nine tenths of the population of the
country'.

These differences in attitude to St Patrick's Day became
much greater after 1921. In the south St Patrick's Day was
made a general holiday and from 1925 all public houses were
closed on that day. An annual army parade now replaced the

processions organised by the lord lieutenant and lord mayor in Dublin. Throughout the country there were processions, usually including army marches to church for mass. The Irish language was promoted, often with events organised by the Gaelic League. In 1926 the southern premier William Cosgrave, made the first official radio broadcast on St Patrick's Day, stating that the destiny of the country, north and south, was now in the hands of Irishmen and urging toleration.[20] With the accession to power of Eamon de Valera and Fianna Fáil in 1932 the day took on added significance. Links between church and state were publicly emphasised by the annual procession on St Patrick's Day of de Valera and his cabinet, complete with a cavalry troop, to the pro-cathedral for mass.[21] The Patrician Year of 1932, which included the Eucharistic Congress, gave an opportunity for large demonstrations emphasising connections between Ireland and Rome, a subject which de Valera would return to in his St Patrick's Day broadcast of 1935 in which he reminded people that Ireland had been a Christian and catholic nation since St Patrick: 'she remains a catholic nation'.[22] De Valera now used the St Patrick's Day broadcasts, which were transmitted to the USA and Australia, to launch vigorous attacks on the British government and partition. These speeches reached a peak in 1939, when in Rome de Valera declared how he had pledged himself 'beside the grave of the great Hugh O'Neill never to rest until that land which the Almighty so clearly designed as one shall belong undivided to the Irish people' and he urged his listeners to do likewise.[23]

In Northern Ireland St Patrick's Day continued to be observed but on a lower key than in the south. Newspaper reports during the 1920s and 1930s indicate that the shamrock was still worn widely on St Patrick's Day, which remained a bank holiday when banks, government and municipal offices, and schools were closed, although most shops and factories seem to have been unaffected.[24] In catholic churches it remained an important feast day which was well attended. The Ancient Order of Hibernians continued to organise demonstrations on this date. The Patrician Year of 1932 was marked by all the churches, but especially by the

catholic church and the Church of Ireland.[25] At Saul, the site
of Patrick's first church, the Church of Ireland built a new
church while the catholic church erected a statue of St
Patrick on a nearby hill top. Sporting activities on St Patrick's
Day, most notably the Ulster schools rugby cup, and special
theatrical events were well attended, while from 1925 BBC
(Northern Ireland) commenced an annual series of special
St Patrick's Day broadcasts.[26] In 1980 the journalist Norman
Ballentine remembered some of the traditions associated
with St Patrick's Day in the 1930s: 'Every St Patrick's Day we
would crowd the terraces of Ravenhill for the Schools' Cup
Final, and in the evening would gallop up miles of stone steps
to the gods in the Opera House for a variety show in which
the comediens were all primed as to the local importance of
the day and came out with corny jokes about Methody and
Inst.'[27] Special ceremonies of the trooping of the colour and
presentation of the shamrock to Irish regiments remained a
tradition. But, apart from a brief effort by the Duke of
Abercorn, when governor of Northern Ireland, to run a government ball in the evening, there was no official involvement in or recognition of St Patrick's Day.

After the second world war, celebration of St Patrick's Day
continued to be marked very differently in the two parts of
Ireland. In 1950 the military parade in Dublin was replaced
by a trade and industries parade. Recently, another journalist
Nuala O'Faolain has recalled this occasion from the 1950s:

> It was never what was in the parade that mattered. It was going to
> the parade. Going into town on the bus. Wearing your green
> rosette. Town being different. Everything lasted for ages,
> because of the multiplicity of bread vans ... Year after year, runny-
> nosed children in parkas were hoisted on to shoulders to admire
> the ATA Alarm float.[28]

Dances, sporting activities, theatrical events and excursions
were run on the day. Not only heads of government, such as
de Valera and Costello, but ministers such as Séan MacEntee
and James Ryan used the event to make strong denunciations
of partition, especially in the late 1940s and 1950s.[29]

Newspaper headlines of 'church and state unite' reported military church parades with associated civilian processions in many parts of the country, while leaders such as Costello in their speeches emphasised links between Ireland and Rome.[30] The 1961 Patrician celebrations marked a high spot in this religious aspect of the festival. It began with the arrival on 13 March of a papal legate, Cardinal MacIntyre, who in the words of the *Capuchin Annual* was 'welcomed with the protocol reception given only to a head of state,' which included a welcome from the Taoiseach and a full military guard.[31]

In the north, after the war, banks and government offices continued to close on St Patrick's Day, while the wearing of the shamrock remained popular and the tradition of presenting it to Irish regiments was continued. Catholic churches still observed it as a special feast-day, and the Ancient Order of Hibernians kept it as a date for parades and demonstrations. But for many areas of work and activity, the press by the 1950s reported 'business as usual', and many schools seemed to have dropped it as a day of holiday by the early 1960s.[32] Correspondents in the newspapers decried the political way in which it was celebrated in the south.[33] A government information officer in the late 1950s urged that it might be wise 'quietly to forget St Patrick's Day' but this was rejected.[34] At the same time, we may note that there were those in unionist and protestant church circles who believed that more attention should be given to the event. From the mid 1950s the editorial in the *Belfast Telegraph* urged on a number of occasions that the day should be a full public holiday, a request backed by the Church of Ireland diocesan synod of Down and Dromore.[35] In the late 1950s and 1960s the Church of Ireland inaugurated a pilgrimage and special service in Downpatrick and Saul to which the Archbishop of Canterbury, Dr Ramsey, was invited in 1964. This event was the occasion of one of the first ecumenical gestures when the local nationalist councillors turned up to greet the archbishop at the cathedral, although they felt unable to attend the service.[36]

From the early 1970s celebration of St Patrick's Day changed considerably, especially in the republic. The most conspicuous change was in the character of the Dublin parade after its organisation was taken over in 1970 by Dublin Tourism. There were now bands and majorettes as well as many tourists from the USA and Canada in the parade, which took on a new tourist and commercial aspect. More significant changes, however, occurred in other areas. An editorial in the *Irish Independent* on 16 March 1974 pointed out that since the troubles had begun in the north, speakers at St Patrick's Day parades had become more sensitive about their words and there was a growing acceptance of different traditions in Ireland. Speeches by leading politicians no longer contained strong condemnation of partition, and, especially in the USA, Irish government ministers often denounced violence and support for the IRA.[37] On a religious level, efforts were also made to overcome the denominational divisions associated with the saint's day. On St Patrick's Day 1972 Father Michael Hurley, S.J., became the first catholic priest to preach in St Patrick's Cathedral, Dublin, since the Reformation. Interdenominational services were now regularly held on the day and an ecumenical blessing of the shamrock at the G.P.O. became a regular feature of the Dublin parade.[38] A new organisation was set up in 1995 to run the Dublin parade which has now become part of an all-day cultural and tourist festival. The chairman Michael Colgan has declared: 'We are looking to make this a national day of celebration'. On the new parade he has commented: 'the day is long gone when you could have an electrical company with washing machines on a float and a girl in a sash'.[39]

In Northern Ireland there were also changes in the way that St Patrick's Day was celebrated. During the 1970s and 1980s renewed interest in the festival was apparent in catholic circles. The year 1974 saw a St Patrick's Day parade on the Falls Road in Belfast, and three years later there was a parade in Derry, revived after twenty-five years.[40] A.O.H. parades continued on the day, as did catholic-organised parades in centres like Armagh. New civic organised parades were held in Newry, Downpatrick and elsewhere. The shamrock continued to be presented to soldiers at St Patrick's Barracks, Ballymena. Protestant interest in St Patrick's Day was still expressed in support for the Ulster Schools Rugby Cup final and for Church of Ireland services at Downpatrick and Armagh. During the 1980s there seems to have been a slight renewal of interest in St Patrick's Day among protestants. In 1985 Belfast Orangemen took part in a St Patrick's Day parade along the Shankill and Newtownards Roads; in 1990 members from Belfast joined brethren of Ballymena St Patrick's Church Orange Lodge at their annual church service; and in 1994 St Patrick's flag flew over the Orange headquarters in Belfast for the first time on 17 March.[41] The 1980s and 1990s witnessed growing interdenominational co-operation on St Patrick's Day. The first joint protestant/catholic service in Down Church of Ireland cathedral was held on 17 March 1985 while on 17 March 1990 in Armagh catholic cathedral an ecumenical service commemorated the laying of the cathedral foundation stone in 1840.[42] A special ecumenical service was held in Downpatrick for victims of violence on St Patrick's Day 1994. At the Armagh celebrations in 1995 the customary catholic procession was joined by protestant boy scouts for the first time.

Commemoration of St Patrick's Day has not been confined to Ireland. In 1713 in his journal to Stella, Jonathan Swift remarked that on St Patrick's Day in London the Mall was so full of crosses (a reference to St Patrick's Cross) that he 'thought all the world was Irish'.[43] Celebration of St Patrick's Day in the American colonies was first recorded in 1737 in Boston and in New York in 1762.[44] These occasions took the form of dinners, the people originally involved being all Irish protestants who were loyal to the crown, and the toasts included 'the glorious memory of King William'. During the first half of the nineteenth century St Patrick's Day continued to be celebrated at annual dinners, attended by well-to-do protestant and catholic American citizens of Irish extraction. In the quarter-century after 1850, however, the whole character of these celebrations changed dramatically. In the years following the Great Famine very large numbers of poor catholic Irish arrived in New York and other east-coast cities,

where they often faced deep local hostility and discrimina-
tion. On St Patrick's Day parades were now organised
which served as a focus for the exhibition and definition of
a new Irish-American identity which was strongly nationalist. St Patrick's Day parades became an important annual
event in the life of the Irish catholic community in America
from the 1850s onwards, because they met the *present* needs
of that community in a hostile world. It was, in the words of
one American historian, 'a mass ritual which symbolically
acted out Irish respectability in the face of hostility and
Irish unity in nationalist terms'.[45]

These parades seem to have become largely associated
with the Irish catholic American community rather than
the Irish protestant American community, probably
because the latter group were less conscious of religious
and social alienation from the broader American society.
In some areas celebration of St Patrick's Day remained
non-political and non-denominational, but in important
centres like New York and Boston the parades were a
reflection of the growing political strength of Irish
catholic America.[46] These parades have continued
throughout the twentieth century, even though the
social and economic circumstances of Irish catholic
Americans have improved dramatically. In multi-ethnic
America, Americans of Irish background now celebrate
St Patrick's Day to mark out their own separate ethnic
background.[47] In 1983 it was reckoned that 14 million
St Patrick's Day cards were posted in the USA.[48] Most
controversy in recent years has surrounded the New York
St Patrick's Day parade (controlled by officials of the
A.O.H. since the 1850s), where political reverberations of
the northern conflict have been felt. In 1994, reflecting the
importance of American catholics of Irish descent,
President Clinton had a special St Patrick's Day party in the
White House.[49] Even though he is a protestant of Irish
background, apparently no unionists or representatives
of protestant Irish America were invited. In 1995, however,
the guest list did include protestants and unionists from
Northern Ireland.[50]

II

For many years Easter Sunday has been the focus of commemoration for the Easter Rising of 1916. At present, however, this event is no longer marked in a major way in Dublin, even though the rising was centred in Dublin and on many occasions in the past the city has witnessed significant celebrations at Easter to mark this event. Official involvement on an annual basis in this commemoration began only in 1954. In recent years there have been large commemorations to mark the Easter Rising in West Belfast although Belfast was not involved in the rising and indeed West Belfast was the scene of Sinn Fein's greatest defeat in the subsequent general election of 1918 when the Sinn Fein leader Eamon de Valera was beaten at the polls by the constitutional nationalist Joseph Devlin.

In the years immediately after the rising there was little sign of annual commemoration, mainly no doubt because of British government restrictions.[51] At Easter 1922, there were commemorations in a number of towns where prominent politicians from both the pro-treaty and anti-treaty sides addressed large crowds. In the following year the event was not marked, owing to the civil war. In 1924 the anniversary took on a new form in the shape of a march to Glasnevin cemetery for the laying of wreaths on the republican plot. This event was organised by republicans, and the Free State government took no part in it. In following years a similar pattern was followed and large parades organised and attended by republicans took place through Dublin to Glasnevin. They contained many different republican groups including Sinn Fein and (after 1927) Fianna Fáil. The Cumann na nGaedheal government did not participate in these marches, although there was some official remembrance of the Easter Rising in 1926 and after in the form of broadcasts on the subject on the new Radio Éireann. Most official emphasis in this period went into St Patrick's Day, with its many parades and army involvement.

When Fianna Fáil came to power in 1932, this situation changed little. In Dublin there were two parades, the first organised by the semi-official National Commemoration

Committee and attended by de Valera and Fianna Fáil T.D.'s
which marched to Arbour Hill, where the executed 1916
leaders had been buried, and the second organised by other
republican groups, including the I.R.A., which marched to
Glasnevin. In 1935 there was a large Irish army parade on
Easter Sunday to the G.P.O. where a statue of Cuchulainn was
unveiled and speeches were made by government ministers.
After 1935 the event reverted in Dublin to commemoration
in the form of the two rival marches to Arbour Hill and
Glasnevin. Anthony Butler has recalled these parades in the
1930s:

> Easter parades to Glasnevin cemetery were [...] occasions when
> disturbances arose. To add fuel to an already explosive fire, mem-
> bers of the communist party of Ireland - all twenty-eight of them
> - would fall in uninvited behind the I.R.A. ranks and display con-
> spicuous red rosettes in their buttonholes. This rearguard was
> understandably subject to angry attacks by citizens gathered
> along the route.[52]

For the Fianna Fáil government also St Patrick's Day
remained the most important event for official marches and
political speeches. Outside Dublin the Rising was commemorated by competing republican bodies.

In the north the efforts to commemorate the 1916 rising at
Eastertime were low-key and sporadic until the end of the
1920s, when meetings were planned at Milltown cemetery in
Belfast and Derry city cemetery, only to be banned by government order.[53] Every Easter during the 1930s similar meetings were announced and then banned, but there usually
followed attempts by demonstrators to evade the ban.[54] In
Belfast people would gather at the grounds nearest to
Milltown cemetery, and a decade of the rosary would be
recited there. In a number of places, such as Armagh, wreaths
would be laid on republican graves on Easter Saturday before
the ban came into force on Easter Sunday. In Derry demonstrators held brief public meetings in different locations to
outwit the authorities. In Newry a service was held in the
church adjacent to the republican plot and people at the ser-

vice would go afterwards to the graves. In Northern Ireland tension arose over the flying of the tricolour and the wearing of the Easter lily. Greatest confrontation between the police and republican organisers came during the war, when active I.R.A. units became involved in the event in 1942, leading to shooting and the death of a police constable and the wounding of other policemen.[55]

In 1941, on the twenty-fifth anniversary of Easter week, major celebrations were held in Dublin. On Easter Sunday there took place what the *Irish Independent* called, 'the largest and most spectacular military parade the city has seen' with 10,000 others from various groups taking part.[56] There were speeches at the G.P.O. from President Douglas Hyde and members of the government. One newspaper correspondent in his report of the military parade described 'the gay clatter of regimental bands playing unceasingly, armoured cars nozzling by to a marching version of the Londonderry air: Ireland 1941 - soldiers in field green, regiments of nurses in black stockings and white gloves - an entire nation prepared.'[57] De Valera made a broadcast calling for improvements in the arms forces and for vigilance to preserve Ireland's independence. Some have seen the whole occasion as having been used 'as a rallying point for the nation and was a direct response to the threats to Ireland's neutrality by the second world war'.[58] During the remainder of the war no celebrations occurred. When they recommenced after 1945 they continued to be marked by rival parades, with no special government involvement, apart from the appearance of Fianna Fáil ministers at Arbour Hill. In 1949, no doubt for symbolic reasons, the official inauguration of the Irish republic occurred at one minute past midnight on Easter Monday.

An annual military parade on Easter Sunday commenced only in 1954.[59] It was part of the An Tóstal celebrations of that year but was continued in following years. The fortieth anniversary of the rising was celebrated extensively in 1956.[60] In addition to the military parade in Dublin where the President, Seán T O'Kelly, the Taoiseach, John A. Costello and other government ministers were on the saluting platform at the G.P.O., there were many radio programmes on the rising, and various groups in different parts of the country held parades. After this the commemoration returned to the practice of a military parade in Dublin and other marches in Dublin and elsewhere organised by various republican groups.

The fiftieth anniversary of the Easter Rising in 1966 was the occasion of widespread ceremonies.[61] In the south there were events during the whole of Easter week. On the Sunday there was a large parade in Dublin led by units of the Irish army and including Old I.R.A. members. A special broadcast was made from the G.P.O.. A separate republican-organised parade was held to Glasnevin. On Easter Monday President de Valera opened the Garden of Remembrance in Parnell Square, dedicated to all those who gave their lives for Irish freedom. Outside Dublin there were many special ceremonies to mark the occasion. After 1966 celebrations of the rising returned to their previous pattern of Easter Sunday parades. The outbreak of violence in Northern Ireland cast a shadow over these commemorations. In 1972 the military parade in Dublin was cancelled, and there were two brief ceremonies, one at the G.P.O. and the other at the Garden of Remembrance.[62] There are no longer major official ceremonies, although there are usually some gestures of commemoration, such as a ceremony at Arbour Hill. Special dates, like the seventy-fifth anniversary in 1991, have passed with little note, official or otherwise, in the south.[63]

In 1948 the government ban in Northern Ireland on Easter Sunday parades or meetings was lifted. In 1950 the event at Milltown cemetery in Belfast was marked by services held by three different organisations, the National Graves Association, the Irish Labour Party and the Old I.R.A..[64] During the 1950s and 1960s there would often be several organisations involved at Milltown. In 1950 and subsequent years, the Easter Sunday commemoration parade in Newry included members of Newry urban council, the Foresters and the Hibernians, while parades were also organised in Derry and at other centres throughout Northern Ireland.[65] During the 1960s marches continued to be held with few problems, although sometimes there was conflict between organisers and police over the flying of the tricolour. The fiftieth anniversary of the rising was the occasion of considerable commemoration in the north, especially in Belfast.[66] On Easter Sunday there was a parade to Milltown, while on the following Saturday, 16 April, there was the main procession to Casement Park, where a meeting was held. A march to protest at republican parades was also organised on 16 April, but there was only minor conflict between the two. There were parades or commemorations elsewhere during this week. In the early 1970s there were once again several parades to Milltown, organised by both provisional Sinn Féin and official Sinn Féin. [67] Easter Sunday now became the occasion for large republican demonstrations in the north. The sixty fifth anniversary of the Easter Rising in 1981, during the hunger-strike, saw widespread protest marches.[68] Easter Sunday continues to be an important day of commemoration among northern republicans.[69]

III

At present the twelfth of July is the occasion of a public holiday in Northern Ireland. On that day the victory of King William III at the Battle of the Boyne in 1690 is remembered. It is marked by Orange parades held in many parts of Northern Ireland. Before the 1790s, as Jacqueline Hill has pointed out 'liberals and even radicals revered William' because of his ideas of civil liberty and religious toleration, but he now became exclusively a protestant hero.[70] One hundred years after the Battle of the Boyne the event was hardly noted at all in the north of Ireland. While there were celebrations of the centenary of the battle in Dublin and in some other parts of Ireland, the only instances of public remembrance in Ulster seem to have been two dinners at Doagh (Co. Antrim) and Downpatrick (Co. Down) where toasts to King William were followed by other favourite toasts of reformers, such as the Irish Volunteers and the American Revolution.[71] The Orange Order, founded in 1795, did make a central point of celebrating the Boyne anniversary, but this organisation and its July celebrations did not achieve mass support among Ulster protestants until the last decades of the

nineteenth century. The twelfth of July became a bank
holiday only in 1925 in Northern Ireland.

The twelfth of July 1796 saw the first Orange demonstrations on the anniversary of the Boyne with the main parades
being held in Lurgan, Portadown and Waringstown.[72] The
Orange Order had been founded in September 1795 after a
clash at a place called The Diamond, near Loughgall, Co.
Armagh, between members of opposing agrarian societies,
namely the Peep O'Day Boys (protestants) and Defenders
(catholics).[73] Members of the former group established the
Orange Society as a popular, exclusively protestant organisation which quickly spread beyond Co. Armagh and which was
based on local lodges with a structure of district lodges,
county lodges and a grand lodge. Its name referred to
William's title as prince of Orange. Over the next three
decades, as new Orange lodges were founded, twelfth of July
celebrations spread to many areas, especially, but not exclusively, in Ulster. The *Belfast Newsletter* on 16 July 1805
described an Orange parade in Belfast on 12 July to a church
service, afterwhich the marchers adjourned to lodge rooms
'where the evening was spent with the greatest harmony and
conviviality'. The minute book of the Aughnacloy Orange
Lodge in Co. Tyrone recorded on 12 July 1802 that the
brethren consumed 4 quarts and one pint of rum, 1 ½ pints
of spirits, 2 pints of port wine, 7 quarts of beer and 4 quarts
of punch.[74] The *Belfast Newsletter* in 1822 reported that on the
12th of July over a hundred lodges marched through
Dungannon while in Enniskillen, where Orange flags were
exhibited and an arch was constructed over the bridge, several local lodges processed through the town, after which
'they separated for their respective dinner rendezvous, in a
sober and peaceable manner, having neither given nor
received offence'.[75] Not all such parades ended peacefully,
however, and were often the occasion of disorder or of conflict between Orangemen and local catholics.[76]

The government's attitude to the parades and the
Orangemen changed. At the beginning the authorities
looked favourably on the twelfth of July anniversary. Their
response began to alter in the early decades of the nineteenth

century, however, because the parades often led to disturbances, and increasingly the authorities sought to adopt a
neutral stance on such commemorative events and demonstrations.[77] An 1823 act aimed at curbing popular societies in
Ireland (including Daniel O'Connell's Catholic Association)
was the first of a number of government measures which
affected the Orange Order and its parades. But while these
efforts were successful in Dublin, the twelfth of July parades
continued in parts of Ulster. The Anti-Processions Act of
1832, however, did have the desired effect in curbing these
marches. In some areas the ringing of bells and the holding
of private dinners on the twelfth of July continued, but the
authorities took action against those who continued to
parade. A police report from Co. Monaghan on 12 July 1834
recorded: 'Monaghan, a procession; some armed; all tranquil, 12 identified. Castleblayney, a procession of 40 persons,
one sword was taken by order of Mr Wally, a magistrate; dispersed quietly'.[78] After the Anti-Processions Act was lifted in
1845 there were once again many twelfth of July processions.[79] Confrontation between Orangemen and catholics
still occurred, however, and after a large scale fight at Dolly's
Brae near Castlewellan, Co Down, on 12 July 1849, which left
a number of catholics dead, the government introduced in
1850 a new Party Procession Act which forbade public dis-
plays or demonstrations.[80]

This 1850 act (strengthened by the 1860 Party Emblems
Act) made the public commemoration of the Boyne very difficult. The authorities took action against those who broke
the law. In 1863, for example, it was reported in the local
press that in Gilford, Co. Down, eight millworkers were
arrested for 'parading behind fifes and drums when leaving
work on 14 July', while three years later three men were
arrested in the Portadown area 'for meeting and parading in
the public road, wearing party colours, and playing music,
which was calculated to provoke animosity between different
classes of Her Majesty's subjects'.[81] On 12 July 1867 William
Johnston of Ballykilbeg, Co. Down, challenged the ban by
leading a large parade of Orangemen from Newtownards to
Bangor.[82] He was arrested, tried and imprisoned in

Downpatrick jail. He emerged from jail to become a great
Orange hero, was elected M.P. for Belfast, and was responsible for having the Party Processions Act repealed in 1872.
Subsequently the 1870s and 1880s witnessed extensive twelfth
celebrations. The 1873 Canadian Orangemen joined the
parades in Ulster, a reflection of how the Orange Order and
its celebrations of the Boyne event were now found in many
parts of the world[83]; for example, it has been estimated that
by the 1870s about one-third of all adult male protestants in
Canada were active or former members of the Order.[84] The
political controversy over home rule in the last two decades of
the nineteenth century gave considerable impetus to the
twelfth celebrations in Ulster, which became a focal point for
unionist opposition to home rule.

During the nineteenth century these Orange twelfth of
July celebrations underwent considerable change. The
appearance of the parades altered markedly. Coloured
sashes emerged in the early 1800s and were worn across the
shoulder; by the late nineteenth century these were being
replaced by a collarette type of sash, worn originally in
indoor functions.[85] In the early period fife-and-drum bands
provided the marching music, while flute bands only
appeared commonly in the last decades of the century and
the introduction of accordian, silver and pipe bands belong
to the early twentieth century. The Lambeg drum seems to
date from this later period.[86] Early flags and banners featured little more than embroidered pictures of King
William and the reigning sovereign, and it was not until the
late 1870s and 1880s that we find banners with a greater
variety of painted scenes, including historical and scrip-
tural subjects.[87] Strong efforts to avoid disturbance and
control drinking were made in the later period. William
Johnston, for example, promoted temperance and total
abstinence lodges, while the minutes of the Co. Tyrone
Mountjoy Faith Defenders Orange Lodge in 1892 declared
that 'no person be allowed to walk if they be under the
influence of drink.'[88] Early in the twentieth century
attempts would be made to have public houses closed on
the twelfth of July.[89]

Important social and political changes occurred in regard to the parades in the last three decades of the nineteenth century. The size of the demonstrations increased considerably, not only because of the growing number of Orangemen, but also because the development of the railways meant that people from a wide areas could be more easily brought together.[90] As a result, twelfth of July demonstrations were no longer small localised affairs. In the early parades the Orangemen were largely drawn from the labouring and small-farmer classes, and this seems to have remained the case until the last decades of the nineteenth century.[91] Gentry participation, evident earlier on, had decreased by the 1870s.[92] During the 1880s, however, particularly from 1885-6 when the home rule crisis emerged to the fore of politics, growing numbers of gentry, well-to-do tenant farmers and professional people joined the Order and the parades.[93] Members of the Church of Ireland had predominated in earlier years but now large numbers of presbyterians took part in the twelfth celebrations.[94] The parades assumed a much more important role, when, from the early 1880s, it became customary for politicians to address the assembled marchers: from 1885 onwards, of course, important links were established between the Orange Order and the new unionist party. From the 1870s, the passing of resolutions, on both political and religious matters, became common practice at the 'field.[95]

In the early 1900s, however, social and religious division within the Orange Order led to the founding in 1903 of the Independent Orange Order which mounted its separate July anniversary parades. Under the influence of R. L. Crawford the new organisation issued in July 1905 its Magheramorne manifesto which proclaimed that the new order,

> once more stood on the banks of the Boyne, not as victors in the fight nor to applaud the noble deeds of our ancestors .... but to .... hold out the right hand of friendship to those who, while worshipping at other shrines, are yet our countrymen - bone of our bone, bone of our flesh.[96]

Crawford later adopted a home rule position, for which he was expelled in 1908 and the Independent Orange Order returned to a mainstream unionist stance although it has maintained its independent role to the present day. During the home rule crisis of 1912-14 there continued to be a large turnout of Orangemen at the twelfth of July demonstrations. Celebrations in 1915 were subdued while in 1916, because of the casualties of the 36th (Ulster) Division at the Somme, they were cancelled and church services were held instead. One such service was reported by the *Portadown News*, on 15 July 1916:

> For the first time within the recollection of the oldest Orangeman in Portadown there was no demonstration in con- nection with the anniversary of the Battle of the Boyne, the lodges of the District complying with the request of the Grand Lodge of Ireland that there should be no celebration this year ... There was a large attendance, and the service was of a very solemn and impressive character. The flag of the empire and the flag of Ulster, draped in mourning, were displayed in a promi- nent position in front of the congregation ... In the course of his address Canon Moran paid a warm tribute to the soldiers of the Ulster Division who had fought so valiantly in defence of the flags. [97]

In the early 1920s efforts were made to have 12 July declared a general holiday. At first the new government of Northern Ireland resisted this move. When Sir James Craig was asked in parliament in July 1922 to use his influence to have 12 July proclaimed a general holiday, he stated: 'In view of the large number of existing statutory holidays, and the fact that the 12th of July has for many years been observed as such, there does not appear to be any necessity to take the action suggested'. [98] Three years later, however, it was agreed that the day should be a bank holiday. [99] Contemporary news- paper reports show how during the 1920s and 1930s unionist spokesmen, including most of the government ministers, used in the twelfth platforms to make political speeches. On 12th July 1932 at a demonstration at Poyntzpass, Co. Armagh,

Sir James Craig declared: 'Ours is a protestant government and I am an Orangeman.' A year later at Newtownbutler, Co. Fermanagh, Sir Basil Brooke urged loyalists 'wherever possible, to employ protestant lads and lassies.'[100]

Between the wars, most twelfth of July anniversary commemorations passed off peacefully. On 12 July 1928 the eminent painter Sir John Lavery went to Portadown to paint the local Orange procession (this painting is now in the Ulster Museum). Lavery recorded the event in his diary:

I have seen many processions and exhibitions of intense feeling but nothing to quite equal the austere passion of the Twelfth in Portadown. The colour was more beautiful than anything I have seen in Morocco, black and orange predominating with every other colour except green adding to its beauty and the dozens of big drums beaten with canes by drummers whose lives seemed to depend on the noise they were able to make, their coats off, their shirt sleeves rolled up, their rists [sic] bleeding and a look in the eye that boded ill for any interference...[101]

Sectarian conflict in early 1935 led to concern that the July parades would be the occasion of dangerous confrontation.[102] That year the government banned all parades from 18 June but, in response to strong Orange opposition, it was forced to lift the ban. Processions on the twelfth of July passed off peacefully in most parts of the province. At the close of the Belfast parade, however, serious rioting broke out which continued until the end of August, causing 13 deaths and much destruction. In Cos Donegal, Cavan and Monaghan, Orange parades on the twelfth July continued until 1931, when republicans prevented a parade of the Royal Black Preceptory (a sister organisation of the Orange Order) at Cootehill, in spite of police and soldiers being drafted in.[103] William Cosgrave met a protestant delegation in connection with the matter and stated his support for the right of Orangemen to march but he was unable to guarantee their protection. Henceforth, Orange twelfth of July processions were not held in Cos Cavan or Monaghan; instead joint celebrations with Donegal brethren were organised at Rossnowlagh, Co. Donegal.

During the second world war, 12th of July processions were suspended. After the war, the marches returned to their normal pattern. The occasion was used frequently for speeches attacking the southern government and denouncing the catholic church.[104] The twelfth parades continued to attract large crowds. A newspaper report of the Armagh county demonstrations in 1951 in Portadown noted that 'one hundred and twenty specially chartered buses will be in operation, while seven special trains are being run. In addition many others will arrive by car and other means of transport.[105] Parades in this post-war period mostly passed off without trouble. Traditional routes seem to have helped avoid friction. Conflict broke out in Annalong, Co. Down, however, over an Orange proposal to march along the Longstone Road, which was not a traditional route and went through a catholic area.[106] Government attempts in 1952 and on later occasions to impose a ban on this route aroused strong criticism of the government from the Orange Order and some unionist MPs.

The outbreak of the 'troubles' in 1969 did not stop the annual celebrations of the anniversary of the Boyne, although in some years, especially in the 1970s, the turnout was lower than usual, because of the disturbed conditions of the time. Since 1969 dispute over marching routes has become a cause of riot and conflict in some areas, especially where there has been a change of population in the area of the route. Recent decades have seen a withdrawal of many of the professional and middle classes from the Orange Order and from participation in the parades, while divisions over various religious and political issues have weakened the impact of the July event. The year 1990 marked the tercentenary of the Battle of the Boyne. Figures for Orange membership in that year in Ireland were put at close to 100,000 in a total of 1,400 lodges, all of which were in Northern Ireland except for small numbers in Leitrim, Wicklow, Cavan, Monaghan and Donegal; in Scotland Orangeism has a substantial membership while outside the British Isles Orangeism has its strongest base in Canada with about 25,000 members.[107] The tercentenary year was marked not only by large demonstrations on the twelfth, but also by pageants re-enacting the Boyne and by other events, including the issue of a special commemorative stamp by the Irish government. In recent years there has been considerable debate as to how far the July anniversary celebrations should be treated as a political, religious or cultural event.[108]

IV

Remembrance Sunday in November commemorates the many men and women who served and died in the British and allied forces in the two world wars. Originally Armistice Day on 11 November (the official date of the end of the first world war) was the day on which they were remembered, but after the second world war this event was moved to the Sunday nearest to Armistice Day. This special day at present is marked principally in Northern Ireland, and largely by members of the protestant population. Over the last half-century this event has been commemorated by relatively few in the Republic of Ireland. Yet, a majority of those Irishmen who died came from the catholic community throughout Ireland. This includes not only the first world war when all of Ireland was part of the United Kingdom but also the second world war when volunteers from the south as well as Irish in Great Britain served in crown forces. In the second world war one Victoria Cross was awarded to a northern catholic James Magennis, while four Victoria Crosses were awarded to men from the south. Yet until recently councillors or M.P.s from the Social and Democratic Labour Party have not taken part in Remembrance Day ceremonies in Northern Ireland. How Ireland has commemorated its war dead is the subject of important research by Dr Keith Jeffery and Jane Leonard.[109]

The first anniversary of Armistice Day in Ireland, 11 November 1919, was widely observed throughout the country. In Dublin the *Irish Times* 12 November 1919, reported that:

'The two minutes' silence in recognition of the first anniversary
of Armistice Day proved a markedly impressive event in Dublin
yesterday. When the eleventh hour of the eleventh day of the
eleventh month was chimed, a calm and stillness pervaded the
entire city that was manifestation of the feelings of the people in
regard to the solemnity of the occasion. The spontaneous manner in which the citizens responded to the desire of the King was
alike admirable and creditable. Not a sound was heard during
the brief period allotted for uniting in the simple service of
silence and remembrance; vehicular traffic ceased as if by clock-
work on the eleventh hour being tolled; work in all big industrial
concerns, commercial establishments, public offices, and places
of business were suspended; trains ceased running on the various
railway systems; pedestrians stood still on the footpath with hats
doffed and heads reverently bowed, and in all other departments
of work-a-day life the same regard for the solemnity of the occasion was observed.

In Belfast the *Irish News* on the same day, described how 'the
two minute pause was generally observed in Belfast yesterday
... on the lines suggested by the King, all work in the shops
and factories and all traffic in the streets being stopped at
11 o'clock for the space of two minutes.' Services were held
in most churches, north and south. From the beginning of
the 1920s the event was marked not only with a two minute
silence and church services, but with parades or large gath-
erings around recently unveiled war memorials.

In the south, republican opposition to the war and to the
British link lead to the contesting of this event of commemoration. Throughout the 1920s and 1930s, however, Armistice
Day witnessed major assemblies or parades in Dublin. Large
numbers gathered at College Green or St Stephen's Green
where remembrance ceremonies took place.[110] As in Britain
war veterans were initially divided between the various organisations, reflecting different political traditions, but most had
come together in the mid 1920s under the British Legion. In
this first decade after the war, large numbers of poppies were
sold in Dublin and the union jack was well in evidence on the
day. Outside of Dublin there were various ceremonies on

Armistice Day, such as an assembly on 11 November 1924 of 500 ex-servicemen in Tipperary.[111] In a limited way the Irish government endorsed these commemorations. A representative from the Cumann na nGaedheal government laid a wreath at the Dublin ceremony from 1924-32;[112] the wreath in 1924 carried an inscription to commemorate 'all the brave men who fell on the field of battle'.[113] This practice ceased when Fianna Fáil came to power in 1932, although a government representative continued to attend the Cenotaph service in London until 1936 (this annual attendance began in 1923). From 1925 the Dublin parade came under pressure from local republican hostility. In that year smoke bombs were hurled at mourners by republicans and the snatching of poppies became a regular occurrence.[114] Because of disruptions over the event, the location for the main commemoration ceremony was moved to Phoenix Park. In the 1930s there was periodic banning of the union jack or legion banners, which featured a union jack, in the parade.[115]

After the government refused to allow the Irish National War Memorial to be erected in Dublin centre, it gave land in 1930 for the memorial to be built, but on the outskirts at Islandbridge. While Fianna Fáil did not send an official representative to the Armistice Day ceremony (held at Islandbridge from 1937 onwards), the government agreed that Eamon de Valera could attend the opening of the memorial but this did not take place due to the outbreak of the second world war.[116] Jane Leonard has described well the growing personal isolation of many of the veterans.

They matured into middle age and retirement, aware that they were excluded from the national cultural identity forged after independence in 1922. This identity declared that:

T'was better to die neath an Irish sky,
Than at Suvla or Sedd el Bahr.

The Irishmen who survived Gallipoli and the Western Front 'had backed the wrong horse in joining the British forces', as one of them recalled. The same veteran recognised that his British Army service was compromised by the Easter Rising and post-war revolution in Ireland but regretted that the history textbooks

used by his children and grandchildren were silent on the extent
of his generation's participation in the war.[117]

   In Northern Ireland commemoration of Armistice Day
developed very differently. As Dr Keith Jeffery has pointed
out, the war, and especially the Somme, was seen by many
unionists as a blood sacrifice for the union, a view not
shared by nationalists.[118] There was some attempt especially
in the early days, to maintain a broad basis for these commemorations. In Ballymena on 11 November 1924 Major
General Sir Oliver Nugent, commanding officer of the 36th
Ulster Division at the Somme, reminded people that service
in the war was given by Ulstermen 'of all denominations and
all classes', and the ceremony for the unveiling of the
Portadown war memorial in the same year involved the
catholic parish priest with other clergy, and wreaths were laid
by representatives of the Orange Order and the Ancient
Order of Hibernians.[119] Before long, however, the occasion
became identified with unionist politics and culture, and
with support for the union and the empire: nationalist
politicians and catholic clergy largely kept away.[120] In some
areas however, especially in garrison towns, the catholic veterans and their families continued to attend armistice ceremonies.[121] The practice in Northern Ireland, as in Great
Britain and the Irish Free State, was for participants to
parade to their respective churches after a commemoration
march and ceremony.
   After the second world war, it was decided to replace
Armistice Day with Remembrance Sunday on the Sunday
nearest to the 11th of November. In Northern Ireland names
of those who had died in the war were added to some memorials. Ceremonies on Remembrance Day continued much as
they had done on Armistice Day, and they remained largely
the concern of the protestant and unionist population. The
sense of alienation felt by catholics was described recently by
Lord Gerry Fitt who had served as a merchant seaman during
the war and who recalled being noticed by some people from
unionist York Street while he was on his way to V.J. celebrations at the Belfast City Hall in 1945:

They weren't too friendly and shouted insults about me being a catholic and Irish neutrality. I remember looking at Union Jacks that were being waved about. I had served under it during the war and had been glad to do so but I realised that here it was a protestant unionist flag and it looked different then.[122]

In some areas, however, such as Strabane, Dungannon and Newry, catholic and protestant veterans joined the ceremonies and marched to their respective churches after the parade.[123] The outbreak of the 'troubles' in 1969 did not prevent commemorations taking place on Remembrance Sunday. At many of these ceremonies tribute has been paid to members of the armed forces who have been killed in the current 'troubles', although the issue of adding their names to the war memorials has been controversial. An atrocity connected with Remembrance Day was the I.R.A. bomb at Enniskillen on that day in 1987 which left 11 dead. In recent decades (as in the early decades of remembrance) catholic clergy such as Canon Hugh Murphy, M.C., a former naval chaplain, have taken an active part in Remembrance Day services and from the early 1990s some S.D.L.P. councillors have attended Remembrance Day ceremonies. In 1995 catholic submariner, James Magennis, the only man from Northern Ireland to win a V.C. in the second world war, was finally honoured in his native city by the placing of his portrait in Belfast City Hall.

During the second world war the south was neutral but many southern Irishmen and women served in the British forces. These included Irish living in Britain and volunteers from the south. The names of those who had died were added to existing church war memorials (although not public memorials) and survivors joined the annual Remembrance Sunday parade in Dublin which marched from the quays to Islandbridge. In 1950 a figure of 3000 was put on the size of the parade.[124] The attitude of the general public towards those who marched remained ambivalent. This annual parade continued until 1970, when it was cancelled by the British Legion on police advice, owing to the northern 'troubles', and the main occasion of commemoration thereafter became an ecumenical service on Remembrance Sunday in St Patrick's Cathedral in Dublin.

In the next decade street sales of poppies halted and many British Legion halls closed, often as a result of attacks.[125] At the same time, many in the republic now began to look at their past in a more pluralist light and started to see Irish involvement in the two world wars in a broader way. In the early 1980s the government sent a minister and senior army officers to the St Patrick's ceremony, in spite of republican opposition.[126] In 1985 a new ceremony was introduced on 11 July at the Garden of Remembrance in Parnell Square to commemorate all Irish who had died in all wars. The main Remembrance Sunday ceremony continues to be held in St Patrick's and the president of Ireland frequently attends. Public revulsion at the I.R.A. bomb at a remembrance day commemoration in Enniskillen in 1987 has 'fuelled a recent desire in the Republic of Ireland to remember the Irish who served in both world wars.'[127] As a result of this change of opinion some British Legion branches have re-opened, a number of war memorials have been repaired and the Irish government maintains the newly restored Irish National War Memorial Park, which was declared formally completed in 1994 after a brief ceremony conducted by a Fianna Fáil minister, Mr Bertie Ahern.[128]

V

Some of the other important dates of annual commemoration in Ireland deserve brief mention. Every year on a Sunday in June in Bodenstown graveyard, Co. Kildare, a number of commemorative ceremonies are held by representatives from various nationalist groupings, ranging from constitutional southern parties to militant republicans. They come to honour Wolfe Tone, the prominent United Irishman, who is buried there and who is regarded as the founder of Irish republican nationalism by them all. As Professor Marianne Elliott has shown, Tone's grave was not an important place of political pilgrimage until 1898, the centenary of the 1798 rising, and he only became the leading historical republican

figure (replacing others such as Robert Emmet) after Patrick
Pearse from 1913 onwards publicly proclaimed Tone,
because of his example and his writings, as the symbol of a
new militant republicanism, of which the outcome was the
1916 rising.[129]

In the 1920s and 1930s the Bodenstown ceremony drew
very large crowds as well as the representatives of the government, the main political parties and various republican and
socialist groups. On 23 June 1924, for example, the *Irish
Independent* reported that: 'A national tribute to the memory
of Wolfe Tone was paid yesterday at Bodenstown. President
Cosgrave, the heads of the Irish army and judiciary and eight
hundred Irish soldiers assembled to do honour to the great
patriot.' This official demonstration was followed by an anti-
treaty republican parade of about 1000 persons. In recent
decades there are no longer such large crowds, but the leaders of the main political groupings, constitutional and revolutionary, still turn up to honour Tone and to make
statements of their beliefs. As Professor Elliott has said, 'Each
takes from the Tone tradition only what it needs to sustain its
own stance.'[130] Selections are made from Tone's writings to
provide backing for arguments on many subjects from physi-
cal force to unity. Over the last century at various periods the
emphasis of the parties on these issues has changed. The
unity of the island of Ireland and the need for republican
unity were often stressed in the 1930s, while Tone's call 'to
substitute the common name of Irishman, in the place of the
denominations of protestant, catholic and dissenter' was not
a common theme until the 1960s.[131]

The dates of 12 and 15 August are the occasion of large
parades every year. On the first date members of the
Apprentice Boys of Derry from various parts of Ulster come
to Derry to parade around the city and sometimes also
around a section of the walls in commemoration of the lifting
of the siege in 1689. Although some sources claim an ancestry for the organisation going right back to the early eighteenth century, in fact the Apprentice Boys Clubs were
founded only in the 1820s after official celebrations of the
siege in the city had ceased. The clubs were formed 'for the

purpose of celebrating the anniversaries of the shutting of
the gates and the relief of Derry, and thus handing down to
posterity the memorable events of the years 1688 and 1689
connected with this city.' [132] Open in theory to all, the membership is in fact restricted to protestants. The organisation
remained a Derry based one until it was transformed in the
1860s. The growth of the railways, especially in 1860 and
1861, providing ease of transport, turned the organisation
from a local movement into a province-wide one. [133] A member of the Apprentice Boys, Councillor Dr Christopher
McGimpsey has recently described the club as an 'over-
whelmingly working-class organisation made up of individuals who believe there are lessons to be learned from the
history of the siege of Derry.' [134] Stronger in small rural towns
and the countryside than in Belfast, the clubs were formerly
associated with the unionist party, but they now contain supporters of various parties.

On the 15th of August every year processions are organised
in several parts of Northern Ireland by the Ancient Order of
Hibernians. This date is a catholic religious festival (the feast
of the assumption of the Blessed Virgin Mary) and the
Hibernians are a fraternal nationalist and catholic organisation. In spite of claims that the movement goes back to Rory
O'More in the seventeenth century, the A.O.H. in fact only
came into existence in Ireland in the nineteenth century. [135]
The A.O.H. was founded in America in the first half of the
nineteenth century by members of an Irish agrarian secret
society called Ribbonmen. Branches were then established in
Ireland in the second half of the century, but A.O.H. parades
on 15 August did not take place until the end of the nineteenth century, although this date had previously been used
often as a religious holiday by catholics. Until 1904, however,
the catholic church looked on the A.O.H. with suspicion
because it was seen as a secret society outside clerical influence, and it was only in that year, thanks to the influence of
Bishop Patrick O'Donnell, that an episcopal ban was lifted. In
1901 membership of the movement was put at only 8,000, but
at its heyday in 1915 it stood at some 122,000, and was found
in many parts of Ireland. The key figure behind this expan-

sion was Joseph Devlin, the leading northern nationalist M.P., who registered the organisation as a friendly society which greatly boosted its membership.[136] The movement had strong links with the nationalist party and it suffered with the decline of that party after 1918. Its parades on 15th August remained major events throughout the 1920s and 1930s, but the activities of the organisation were by this time mainly restricted to Ulster. Thereafter A.O.H. numbers declined, and its membership in 1975 was put at under 10,000.[137]

Besides these annual commemorations or anniversaries, important events or individuals are remembered after a certain period of time. Some of these commemorations are of interest because they did not take place when one might have expected and have occurred only recently. An interesting example is the case of the memorial to the Irish mailboat, the RMS *Leinster*, which was torpedoed by a German submarine in late 1918 with the loss of 501 lives, the worst maritime disaster in Irish history. An outdoor memorial was unveiled only in January 1996. The minister of state for the marine, Mr Eamon Gilmore, officiated at the unveiling ceremony and he posed questions about the failure to commemorate the event until nearly 80 years afterwards:

Was the tragedy of the *Leinster* lost in the euphoria of 'the Armistice' just one month after its sinking? Did it drown in the turmoil of the years after 1918 which led to the establishment of the Irish Free State? Was the new Irish state so anxious to assert its independence from Britain, too uncomfortable with the fact that the vast majority of Irish people who lost their lives on the *Leinster* were wearing the uniform of the British army?[138]

Another case of a change of opinion on the significance of an event relates to the 1798 rebellion. The centenary of the rebellion was widely marked but not among northern protestants and unionists, many of whose ancestors had fought in 1798. In fact a memorial to Betsy Gray, a Co. Down presbyterian rebel heroine, was destroyed in 1898 by her co-religionists. James Mills, who was present at the wrecking of the monument, later described the reasons for their action:

There was to have been a special ceremony at the grave on that Sunday to mark the centenary of the '98 rising and local protestants were inflamed because it was being organised by Roman Catholics and other Home-Rulers. They didn't like these people claiming Betsy, and they became so enraged that they decided to prevent the ceremony from taking place, and they smashed the monument with sledgehammers.[139]

In recent years attitudes on the United Irishmen have changed in the north and they are widely viewed in a positive light. Belfast City Council intends to commemorate the bicentenary of the 1798 rising in 1998. Councillor Fred Cobain, the leader of the council's Ulster unionists, has declared that it is right and fitting that Belfast should celebrate the rising. In an interview in July 1995 he declared:

Belfast at that time was a radical city, influenced by the writings of Thomas Paine and by the French revolution ... Protestants lose out from a lot of history in Ireland because we feel that anything to do with Irish history is anti-unionist and anti-protestant. We have to examine the history and learn the lessons .... The ceasefire has made it easier for people to focus on these issues. When you begin to do this you begin to discover that your perspective isn't a true one. The unionist perspective has been tinged with sectarianism.[140]

Commemorations, festivals and public holidays are an important part of the calendar. A number of these dates recall significant individuals or events from history. As we have seen, there have been many changes in the way in which these occasions have been marked. The role of government and organisations has been influential. Some of these occasions and their related organisations have survived better than others, thanks to the vitality and community links of the organisation involved and the perceived continued relevance of the commemoration. Contemporary concerns have affected how such historical events or people are marked. Often the original date of the subject which is being celebrated is of great antiquity but rarely is there an unbroken line of annual remembrance. These commemorations are often regarded as an integral part of our historical identity but it must be realised how in the intervening period between the original event or individual in the past and our present celebrations there have often been changes, influenced by contemporary events, in the way that these subjects have been recalled. Many of the traditions associated with those commemorations are of recent vintage. This is not to say that such traditions are not meaningful but it does serve to highlight the point that much of the significance of history is due to the way that we receive and understand it rather than it providing a clear and undisputed link with the past.

6

IRISH IDENTITY

The nature and extent of Irish identity has changed
dramatically over the years, owing to the influence of
political, religious and cultural factors. A recent survey
of opinion in Northern Ireland revealed sharp differences
in the community on the question of identity.[1] Of the
protestants questioned, a mere 2 per cent saw themselves
as Irish – the vast majority (nearly 70 per cent) regarded
themselves as British. Of the catholics surveyed a strong
majority (over 60 per cent) described themselves as
Irish. Presumably most people today in the Republic regard
themselves as Irish. This picture will come as no
surprise to most people. The conflict in Ireland is often
interpreted as a deep dispute between protestant unionists
who see themselves as British and catholic nationalists
who see themselves as Irish. However, we must realise
that, historically speaking, the divisions have not
always been as simple as this. In the late 1960s 20 per cent
of Northern Ireland protestants regarded themselves
as Irish. One hundred years ago most protestants
and catholics believed that they were Irish. Two hundred
years ago protestants only were viewed officially as
Irish.

I

In the late eighteenth century, the term, 'the Irish nation' referred usually to those who were involved politically –namely the protestants, in particular the members of the Church of Ireland 'ascendancy' community, whose advantageous position had been reinforced by the penal laws against catholics. Mostly the descendants of English settlers of the late seventeenth and early eighteenth centuries, these protestants in the course of the eighteenth century had come to view themselves as Irish.[2] Professor Thomas Bartlett has remarked: 'In the early part of the eighteenth century, protestants in Ireland disliked being called Irish; by the mid eighteenth-century they objected to people calling them English'.[3] Others, such as presbyterians and catholics, may have felt that they too were Irish, but they were not part of the dominant minority group which controlled political life. Such an élitist view of the 'nation' was commonplace in many countries in contemporary Europe.

In the early nineteenth-century, however, Daniel O'Connell challenged this narrow concept of nationality. He promoted the cause of the catholic majority and insisted that the nation should embrace all the people. For various reasons, not always of his own making, O'Connell's movement resulted in a tendency in some quarters, both protestant and catholic, to associate Irishness exclusively with catholicism and to regard catholics as the 'real Irish', because they were the majority. In his *Memoir on Ireland*, published in 1843, O'Connell himself referred to the catholics of Ireland as 'emphatically the people of Ireland'.[4] One contemporary member of a great ascendancy family, whose life spanned the late eighteenth and early nineteenth- centuries, observed: 'when I was a boy "the Irish people" meant the protestants: now it means the Roman Catholics'.[5]

There were other views on this matter. As early as 1784 the Newry volunteers, in a declaration drafted by William Drennan, announced:

We associate, although differing in religious opinions, because we wish to create that union of power, and to cultivate that brotherhood of affection among all the inhabitants of this island, which is the interest as well as the duty of all. We are all IRISHMEN. We rejoice and glory in that common title which binds us together: and we associate, in order to do everything, that the union of our hearts, and the strength of our hands, can effectuate, to render the name of IRISHMAN honourable to ourselves, serviceable to our beloved country, and formidable to its foes.[6]

In the early 1790s the Society of United Irishmen was founded, with the aim to 'unite the whole people of Ireland, to abolish the memory of all past dissensions and to substitute the common name of Irishman in place of the denominations of protestant, catholic and dissenter'.[7] This approach was later taken up by the Young Irelanders, who were concerned about the view that catholics, as a majority or because of their 'Celtic' roots and catholic religion, constituted the basic Irish nation and in the 1840s they promoted ideas of Irish nationality as embracing everyone who lived in Ireland, irrespective of numbers, creed or origin. Thomas Davis declared that Irish nationality 'must contain and represent the races of Ireland. It must not be Celtic, it must not be Saxon - it must be Irish'.[8] A frequently quoted verse from his poem 'Celts and Saxons' proclaimed:

What matter that at different shrines
We pray unto one God-
What matter at different times
Our fathers won this sod-
In fortune and in name we're bound
By stronger links than steel;
And neither can be safe nor sound
But in the other's weal.

By the second half of the nineteenth century, then, people held various ideas on the question of Irish identity and whom it embraced. On the one hand, there were individuals such as Cardinal Paul Cullen, who believed that Ulster protestants were not Irishmen at all but invaders and interlopers, and

J.G. Biggar, the Belfast-born presbyterian, home rule M.P. for
Co. Cavan, who converted in the 1870s to catholicism which
he saw as the 'national religion'.[9] This viewpoint was enunci-
ated clearly by Father Tom Burke, the popular Dominican
preacher, who declared in 1872: 'Take an Irishman wherever
he is found all over the earth, and any casual observer will at
once come to the conclusion, "Oh, he is an Irishman, he is a
catholic". The two go together'.[10]

On the other hand, there were others, often either liberal,
nationalist or republican in their politics, who took a broader
interpretation of Irishness. Speaking in 1886 John Redmond,
the future leader of the Irish nationalist party, declared:

> By the Irish nation we do not mean any class or sect or creed. By
> Irish independence we mean liberty for every Irishman, whether
> in his veins runs the blood of the Celt or the Norman, the
> Cromwellian or the Williamite, whether he professes the ancient
> faith of Ireland or the newer creed which has given to our coun-
> try some of the bravest and purest of her patriots.[11]

Obviously, protestant home-rulers and nationalists such as
Charles Stewart Parnell and Isaac Butt believed in a broad
interpretation of the Irish nation. Less obviously, the young
protestant and Tory contributors to the *Dublin University
Magazine*, declared their strong attachment to an Irish identity. In the magazine Sir Samuel Ferguson stated his view that
the protestants 'even the newest comers amongst us', pos-
sessed 'as good a claim, now, to the name of Irishman, as had
the Norman invaders to that of Englishmen at the time of the
Edwards'.[12]

How did protestants in Ulster view this matter in the second half of the nineteenth century? The evidence from what
they said and wrote is that they regarded themselves as Irish.
In 1868 William Johnston, the popular Orangeman and M.P.
for Belfast, remarked to a Belfast audience: 'Men must realise
that to be an Orangeman is not to cease to be an Irishman,
having at heart the interests of his country'.[13] In his best-sell-
ing history of the Irish presbyterian church, published in
1886, Dr Thomas Hamilton, later president of Queen's

College, Belfast, described the many different waves of people to invade Ireland and denied that any group had the right
to call themselves 'the real Irish': 'The men of Ulster have just
as much or as little right to call themselves Irishmen as the
men of Munster'.[14]

After the rise of the home rule issue to the forefront of
Irish politics and the emergence of strong nationalist/union-
ist divisions in 1885-6, the language of unionists emphasised
the link with the UK, but this did not destroy their perception
of their Irish identity. For example, in the speeches at the
1892 Ulster unionist convention in Belfast there were numerous references to British citizenship and to the integrity of
the British Isles and Empire; speakers also refered frequently
to their fellow Irish countrymen and to the Irish nation.[15]
The Rev. James Cregan stated: 'I am an Irishman - born in
loyal Belfast'. Some of those present sought to include both
protestant and catholic in their image of Irishness and a
British connection, but others limited it solely to protestants.
A strong regional Ulster consciousness was evident also
among many.

Shortly after the Belfast meeting a convention was held in
Dublin for unionists of the other three provinces. The opening paragraph of their declaration revealed how their unionism was combined with a clear Irish identity.

> We, Irishmen, belonging to the three southern provinces, being
> of all creeds and classes, representing many separate interests,
> and sharing a common desire for the honour and welfare of our
> country, hereby declare our unswerving allegiance to the throne
> and constitution, and our unalterable determination to uphold
> the legislative union between Great Britain and Ireland.[16]

To be Irish in this sense for both southern and northern
unionists was also to be a citizen of the United Kingdom and
the Empire - an attitude similar to that of people in Scotland
who saw themselves as both Scottish and British citizens.[17]
Very rarely do unionists at this time refer to the British nation
or describe themselves as British or Britons; instead they talk
of the Irish nation and of British citizens.[18]

Even in 1912, at the beginning of the crisis over the third home rule bill, we find still a strong sense of Irishness, associated with the British link, among Ulster unionists. At a meeting of women unionists in the Ulster Hall, Belfast, on the 30th September 1912 the chairwoman's speech began with the words:

> We are here because we love our country. We love Ireland. Our greatest desire is that peace and happiness and prosperity should reign throughout the length and breadth of the land. Ours is not a selfish, it is a patriotic policy. We have no ill feeling towards any of our countrymen.[19]

She then proceeded to state their firm commitment to the union between Great Britain and Ireland. A strong Ulster consciousness in this period among northern unionists did not necessarily deny the Irish dimension. In 1912 in parliament T.P. O'Connor questioned Ronald McNeill, later Lord Cushendun, on this point: 'I observe the hon. gentleman called himself an Ulster man. Does he mean by that that he is an Ulster man and not an Irish man?'. McNeill replied: 'I used the expression "Ulster man" as a more particular phrase. Of course I regard myself as being an Irishman'.[20] On a non-political level we may note a resolution passed by the governors of Campbell College, in east Belfast, as late as June 1915, in opposition to the headmaster's efforts to run the school on the lines of an English public school. The resolution began by stipulating that 'Campbell College, founded by an Ulster merchant, is essentially an Irish institution and should primarily aim at satisfying Irish wants and ideals'.[21]

During the critical years 1912-14, we can witness the beginning of a move away from this Irish identity among many Ulster unionists, partly in response to nationalist claims that Ireland as a nation must be independent as a single unit, and partly as a result of growing northern demands that Ulster, or part of it, should be treated separately. We can observe the case of William Moore, M.P. for North Armagh, who referred in 1910 to his parliamentary unionist colleagues 'as Irish unionists, as Ulster unionists', but by 1912 was happy to describe the northern unionist population as part of the British nation.[22] Other M.P.'s, such as James Craig, now emphasised the Ulster aspect. Dr Alvin Jackson has commented: 'For unionists "Ulster" was not only becoming more important than "Ireland" - "Ulster" was becoming institutionally and ideologically an alternative both to Ireland and, indeed, to Britain'.[23]

In the late nineteenth and early twentieth-centuries, the nationalist perspective on being Irish also developed further. The idea of an Irish nation came to be seen as naturally linked to the idea of an independent state in some form or other. With the growth of a heightened sense of 'Irish Ireland', the Irish language and a revival of Gaelic culture became an important part of Irish identity, especially for political nationalists.[24] Some remained keen to keep their sense of Irishness a broad one, irrespective of denominational, social or racial differences. In 1898 John Redmond denounced landlordism but then proceeded to say:

> After all, these landlords are Irishmen ... While we have waged a war against a system, I believe the great bulk of the Irish people never at any time desired to drive any class of their fellow countrymen from the shores of Ireland.[25]

In his book *Home life in Ireland,* published in 1909, Robert Lynd, asked: 'what is an Irishman?' In reply to his own question, he stated:

> The truth is, there is a great deal of nonsense talked about 'the real Irishman and the typical Irishman' – to mention two phrases common among thoughtless people. The real Irishman is neither essentially a Celt nor essentially a Catholic. He is merely a man who has had the good or bad fortune to be born in Ireland or of Irish parents, and who is interested in Ireland more than any other country in the world. The Orange labourer of the north, whose ancestors may have come from Scotland, has all the attributes of an Irishman no less than the catholic labourer of the west, whose ancestors may have come from Greece, or from Germany, or from Spain, or from wherever you care to speculate.[26]

   Others, however, such as D.P. Moran, emphasised the links between the Irish people and catholicism. Writing in 1901 in *The Leader*, Moran stated:

> The only thinkable solution of the Irish national problem is that one side gets on top and absorbs the other until we have one nation, or that each develops independently. As we are for Ireland, we are in the existing circumstances on the side of catholic development and we see plainly that any genuine non-catholic Irish nationalist must become reconciled to catholic development or throw in his lot with the other side .... If a non-catholic nationalist Irishman does not wish to live in a catholic atmosphere, let him turn Orangeman.[27]

Such views were opposed by people like Douglas Hyde, who in the same year insisted on the 'Davis ideal of every person in Ireland being an Irishman', but, he had to admit, 'it is equally true though, that the Gaelic League and the *Leader* aim at stimulating the old peasant, Papist aboriginal population, and we care very little about the others, though I would not let this be seen as Moran has done'.[28]

   With the quickening of events in Ireland in the years after 1912, owing to armed Ulster unionist resistance to home rule in 1912–14, and the Easter Rising in Dublin in 1916, differences in feelings about Irish identity became more apparent. Concern among Ulster unionists to maintain the constitutional position of the whole of Ireland now changed to a resolve to keep only the province in the union, and finally to a determination to retain just six of the nine counties of Ulster for the link with Great Britain. Among northern unionists there was no understanding of nationalist frustrations, and the 1916 rising was seen simply as a betrayal. Sir Basil Brooke later commented: 'I am not happy about being called an Irishman because of the 1916 rebellion'.[29]

   The 1916 rising was viewed by republicans as an opportunity to affirm the Irish national spirit. The failure of the Irish nationalist party to deal with Ulster unionist opposition was a major factor in the rise of the new republicanism. In a tract *The sovereign people*, published in early 1916, Patrick Pearse wrote of 'Davis's pleas for love and concord between brother Irishmen' as a necessary part of the 'religion of Irish nationality'.[30] But in fact after 1916 the Sinn Féin leaders failed to evolve new policies to cope directly with the situation and instead relied frequently on rhetoric which often reflected narrow attitudes on this question of Irish identity. In 1917 and 1918 Eamon de Valera described the Ulster unionists as a 'foreign garrison' and 'not Irish people'.[31]

II

By 1921 two new political units had emerged in Ireland. For both unionists and nationalists this outcome was very different from the expectations of the pre-1914 period. Only six counties of Ulster, with a substantial catholic minority, remained a part of the United Kingdom, now known as Northern Ireland, while only twenty-six counties, with a small protestant minority, made up the new Irish Free State. In his speech at the opening of the Northern Ireland parliament in 1921, King George V addressed all the people of Ireland:

> The future lies in the hands of my Irish people themselves. May this historic gathering be the prelude of a day in which the Irish people, north and south, under one parliament or two as those parliaments may themselves decide, shall work together in common love for Ireland upon the sure foundation of mutual justice and respect.[32]

Not only did this 'working together' not happen, but in both parts of the divided land the very question of 'the Irish people' would develop significantly and in dramatically different ways.

For the builders of the new southern state, independence had given the opportunity not just to set up an independent government but also to develop an official Irish identity based on some of the 'Irish-Ireland' ideas of the late nineteenth and early twentieth centuries.[33] The Irish language was given a special place in the new state, and the nationalist and republican aspects of Irish history and culture were emphasised not only in the rhetoric and symbols of the new state but also in the school curriculum. Besides making the Irish language compulsory in all schools, the government sought to make it a criminal offence for parents to send their children to schools where Irish was not taught, in the North or in England; legislation was passed to this effect by the Dáil in 1942, but was subsequently overturned in the courts as unconstitutional.[34] In addition, the new Irish national character was often closely associated with catholicism. For example, on St Patrick's Day 1935, de Valera broadcast that Ireland had been a Christian and catholic nation since the time of St Patrick. 'She remains a catholic nation'.[35] The constitution of 1937 declared the nation to be the thirty-two counties of Ireland.

Some southern protestants such as Douglas Hyde were prepared to accept the new Irish ethos, but many were alienated by these new values and emigrated - an important factor in the drop in the protestant population of the twenty-six counties from nearly 10 per cent in 1911 to 7 per cent in 1926 and just 5 per cent in 1960.[36] Other factors also helped this decline, such as the wide distribution of their small numbers and the catholic church's regulations governing mixed marriages. Protestants and former unionists in the south now found themselves described as 'Anglo-Irish'. Lily Yeats, sister of W.B. Yeats, expressed her annoyance at this development: 'We are far more Irish than all the saints and martyrs - Parnell - Pearse - Madame Markieviez - Maud Gonne - de Valera - and no one ever thinks of them as Anglo-Irish'.[37] Even protestant nationalists encountered this problem. Stephen Gwynn, former nationalist M.P. for Galway, remarked in 1926: 'I was brought up to think myself Irish without question or qualification, but the new nationalism prefers to describe me and the like of me as Anglo-Irish'.[38]

What was happening in the north? Just as the independent Irish state developed its sense of Irishness in a largely exclusive way, so in Northern Ireland there was a retreat from a sense of Irishness and the development of a heightened sense of British identity embracing Ulster, or Northern Ireland, which denied increasingly a sense of Irishness. This other exclusive identity, based around unionism, was directed pri-

marily at the protestant section of the population. The
Northern Ireland prime minister Lord Craigavon in 1934
spoke of 'a protestant parliament and a protestant state', and
this spirit affected strongly the new northern identity.[39] British
symbols and culture were emphasised and Irish symbols and
culture were often ignored. For example, Irish history in the
schools and the Irish language were downplayed. The government dropped its grant for the teaching of Irish in schools in
1933, a move welcomed by the *Northern Whig* which referred
to 'moribund Gaelic'.[40] In 1934, after complaints from various
quarters, including Lord Craigavon himself, the B.B.C.
stopped broadcasting Gaelic football results in Northern
Ireland;[41] it recommended in 1946, but initially the results of
matches played on Sunday were broadcast on Monday.

Not part of the new Ulster identity, northern catholics
retained a strong sense of their Irish identity.[42] In spite of its
exclusion from the dominant ethos and political power, the
northern catholic community was large enough to be able to
maintain its own group solidarity around a strong nationalist
and catholic consciousness, unlike the southern protestant
minority whose numbers were much smaller and whose
unionism was now redundant. Organisations such as the
Gaelic Athletic Association and the Ancient Order of
Hibernians, and the catholic school system were important in
maintaining group identity. When the Catholic Truth Society
conference met in Belfast in 1934, the editorial of the *Irish
News* declared:

> North and south are for ever tied by the unbreakable bonds of their
> common Faith, which is their proudest heritage. The ceremonies
> which will take place in Belfast tomorrow, the first day of the
> Catholic Truth Society Conference, will have a northern setting,
> and the majority of the vast multitude worshipping in Beechmount
> will be northern catholics. But the glory will belong to the catholic
> Irish nation ... We leave it to the catholics of Ulster to uphold their
> proud tradition ... Because they are the children of the catholic
> nation which knows of division of soil but not of soul, they will, we
> are sure, demonstrate unswerving loyalty to the faith to which the
> mass rock gives testimony in the dark yesterdays of our history.[43]

The movement in the Ulster protestant community away from an Irish identity did not take place overnight and did not include all protestants. In 1925, in protest at a decision to set up a separate medical register for the south, the Belfast unionist paper the *Northern Whig* declared:

> When Ulster declined to join the south in separating from Great Britain it did not surrender its title as part of Ireland, nor renounce its share in those Irish traditions in art, in learning, in arms, in song, in sport and in science that were worth preserving in a united form.[44]

In many areas and for many unionists this Irish identity survived. For example, the churches, various sporting organisations and some academic bodies maintained their all-Ireland character, and many northern unionists remained happy to call these Irish.

But in other areas this sense of Irishness was fading among the majority of the unionist community. In 1937 the regional director of the B.B.C. for Northern Ireland took exception to a B.B.C. radio feature produced in Manchester called 'The Irish'. He complained that the title was:

> highly undesirable, linking under one name two strongly antipathetic states with completely different political outlooks. There is no such thing today as an Irishman. One is either a citizen of the Irish Free State or a citizen of the United Kingdom of Great Britain and Northern Ireland. Irishmen as such ceased to exist after partition.[45]

Professor J.M. Barkley, in his memoirs, *Blackmouth and dissenter*, has described the events which followed his ordination as a presbyterian minister in 1935:

> Then came the reception in the High Street Café, Ballymoney, the meal being followed by the usual hearty toasts and speeches. The first toast, 'Prosperity to Ireland', was replied to by Mr W.V. McCleery, MP, later minister of Labour and afterwards of Commerce. This toast, normally responded to by a prominent

layman in the local community, remained the custom until about 1937. Following Éire's adoption of a new constitution, some began to use it for party-political purposes, and when Éire became neutral in 1939, the custom fell into desuetude.[46]

The war and the final break between U.K. and the independent Irish state in 1949, following the south's declaration of itself as a republic, was probably another stage in this divergence of identity. In a radio talk on 27 April 1949, Jack Sayers of the *Belfast Telegraph* commented on how with the passage of time since partition matters of identity had changed for many but not all northerners:

What has been the effect of these past twenty-eight years of separation and self-government on people in Northern Ireland? Granted that Ulstermen as a whole are independent and that throughout Irish history they have usually stood by themselves, where is this influence leading? For those who have not ceased to look to Dublin as the capital I can't speak – although it would seem unlikely that there isn't some effect of one kind or another on their minds. Faced with the business of making a living, the contrast in some of the conditions on the two sides of the border must be as apparent to one man as it is to another. Yet no one would suggest that time and circumstance have made them any less Irish.

He then continued:

But is that true of the other body of Ulstermen and women? I have an idea that it is not, and if that is the case, I suggest that it may be one of the most significant facts of our recent history. And today the thought crosses the mind that the appearance of an Irish republic may possibly carry on that whittling down of nationality that has really little to do with politics as we know them. Richard Hayward writes of "An Ulster that remains, say what you will, typically and undeniably Irish in its own Ulster way." The countryside may still be Irish and lots of country people, close to the soil, will not cease to be indigenous, but often I wonder whether those who are more exposed to mass influences aren't becoming more 'Ulster' and less 'Irish' and whether that subtle change isn't still going on.

Sayers acknowledged the change which time had brought:

> The trouble I think, is that the number of those who are equally
> at home in the North or South and who best combine the two in
> themselves is declining. It's almost inevitable that a man from the
> North, without that sense of contact with the rest of the country,
> cannot be as complete an Irishman as his father was in his day.
> Before 1886 the term Ulsterman was probably far less in use than
> it is in 1949.[47]

III

In the late 1960s Professor Richard Rose conducted a survey
of opinion in Northern Ireland about national identity.[48] Of
the protestants 20 per cent saw themselves as Irish, 39 per
cent as British, 32 per cent as Ulster, 6 per cent as sometimes
British and sometimes Irish, 2 per cent as Anglo-Irish while 1
per cent was undecided. Among catholics, the figures were 76
per cent Irish, 15 per cent British, 5 per cent Ulster, 3 per cent
sometimes British, and sometimes Irish and 1 per cent Anglo-
Irish. Clearly this represented a significant change in perception of identity from the beginning of the century. Many
unionists such as Brian Faulkner were still happy to talk of
'fellow Irishmen'. In an article in 1971, Faulkner declared
that, in the same way as Scots can be Scottish and British, 'the
Northern Ireland citizen is Irish and British; it is a question
of complement, not of conflict.'[49] The unionist MP, and
Stormont minister, Dr Robert Simpson, described his nationality in 1970 as follows:

> Certainly we are Irish. When your forefathers have lived in
> Ireland for hundreds of years this is obvious. But we are also
> British. We are United Kingdom citizens paying United Kingdom
> taxes and electing representatives to the United Kingdom par-
> liament.[50]

Ten years after the Rose survey a poll was conducted by
Professor Edward Moxon-Browne. His results showed that
among protestants, those who saw themselves as Irish had
fallen to 8 per cent, in contrast to the greatly increased figure

of 67 per cent for those who choose a British identity and a reduced figure of 20 per cent for those who preferred an Ulster label. For catholics, the figures stood at 69 per cent Irish, 20 per cent British and 6 per cent Ulster. Another survey, conducted in 1989, has confirmed these trends. The percentage of protestants who felt that they were Irish had dropped to 3 per cent, as had those who had chosen Ulster (10 per cent), while a still increasing proportion of 68 per cent called themselves British and 16 per cent described themselves as Northern Irish. Among catholics, those who opted for an Irish label had fallen to 60 per cent, but those who now described themselves as Northern Irish stood at 25 per cent; the figure among catholics for a British identity had fallen to 8 per cent, and for an Ulster identity to 2 per cent. A 1993 survey revealed that among catholics, 12 per cent opted to describe themselves as British, 1 per cent as Ulster, 61 per cent as Irish, and 24 per cent as Northern Irish. For Protestants, 2 per cent saw themselves as Irish, compared with 69 per cent as British, 15 per cent as Ulster, and 11 per cent as Northern Irish.[51]

How exactly matters stand today in regard to issues of identity is unclear, but it is obvious that an acceptance of an Irish identity remains very low among protestants in Northern Ireland. The challenge to unionism from constitutional Irish nationalism and, especially, violent Irish republicanism has helped to diminish further a sense of Irish identity among northern protestants over the last quarter-century. At the same time, various aspects of Irish culture, such as Irish history and language, now have a much greater role than before, both in the schools and in society at large in Northern Ireland. Among northern catholics, Irish identity remains strong.[52] In the republic the last twenty-five years have seen attempts to create a broader, more pluralist sense of Irishness.[53] Abolition of compulsory Irish in many areas, and a greater appreciation of the different strands of Irish history, as seen in official attendances at Remembrance Day services and the removal of some overt Irish/catholic associations, have created a somewhat broader sense of Irishness and Irish identity.

While current attitudes on the question of Irish identity are very polarised, it is worth remembering that there is no permanent, final position on this matter, and that our sense of Irish identity will continue to change in the future. There are signs of interesting developments in this area. In the recent opinion polls considerable support has come from both protestant and catholic communities for the label 'Northern Irish'. In 1993, 24 per cent of catholics and 11 per cent of protestants accepted this description, in comparison with the figures of 20 per cent for catholics and 11 per cent for protestants in 1986, when this category was first introduced.[54] It is not clear how these people would have identified themselves previously but the growing support for this self description is an interesting dimension on Irish identity. In a B.B.C. programme in early 1995 the writer Glenn Patterson stated:

I have no sense of myself as protestant. I do though have some sense of Northern Irishness of which I am proud – Northern Irishness free of political and constitutional absolutes – Northern Irishness in the way that I had of Northern Englishness when I lived in Manchester.[55]

There have been efforts recently from various quarters to remove Irish identity away from a territorial, political framework. During 1993 and 1994, a number of prominent protestants and unionists in Northern Ireland, such as Chris McGimpsey and Sam McAughtry, have called for the promotion of a sense of Irishness, without a political agenda. In an article in the *Belfast Telegraph* of 2 February 1994, Sam McAughtry declared:

I embrace my Irishness and am glad of it. I am a citizen of the United Kingdom and I want to stay that way. I am Irish and I want to stay in the United Kingdom ... We, all of us in Northern Ireland, together with the people of the Republic, are the Irish nation ... We protestants should see ourselves as Irish people with British citizenship. We are a national people, within two national systems ... Unionists, in proclaiming their Irishness, should proclaim also that the Nation and the State need not necessarily be enclosed within the same boundaries ...

Others, such as John Taylor and Ian Paisley, junior, have argued that unionists are not part of the Irish nation but we may note that Rhonda Paisley has been happy to describe herself as an Irishwoman.[56] In his first address as leader of the Ulster unionist party to the party conference in 1995, Mr David Trimble declared: 'The United Kingdom is a genuinely plural state in which it is possible to be Welsh, or Scottish and British. Similarly one can be Irish or Ulster and British as well.'[57]

While this new approach has come from northern unionists, so also there has been a new approach from the south. There have been a number of calls from individuals, such as Mr Dick Spring and Mr Matt O'Dowd, for a more inclusive view of the Irish, nation, including the idea of Irish 'nationism' rather than Irish nationalism.[58] Popular support for a broader concept of Irish identity is seen clearly in the case of the positive public reaction to the Irish football team, whose members are mostly natives of foreign countries, but are labelled as Irish and happily accepted by the population at large. Recent studies of the Irish diaspora, especially Professor Don Akenson's work, have also emphasised the existence of a large number of protestant Irish emigrants, who have a sense of Irish ethnicity, but who do not display strong nationalist political ties.[59] Finally, we may note the call by President Mary Robinson for a broader sense of Irishness in her address to the Houses of the Oireachtas in Dublin on 2 February 1995 on the subject of the Irish diaspora:

Irishness is not simply territorial. In fact Irishness as a concept seems to me at its strongest when it reaches out to everyone on this island and shows itself capable of honouring and listening to those whose sense of identity, and whose cultural values, may be more British than Irish. It can be strengthened again if we turn with open minds and hearts to the array of people outside Ireland for whom this island is a place of origin ... Our relation with the diaspora beyond our shores is one which can instruct our society in the values of diversity, tolerance and fair-mindedness.

To speak of our society in these terms is itself a reference in shorthand to the vast distances we have travelled as a people. This island has been inhabited for more than five thousand years. It has been shaped by pre-Celtic wanderers, by Celts, Vikings, Normans, Huguenots, Scottish and English settlers. Whatever the rights or wrongs of history, all those people marked this island: down to the small detail of the distinctive ship-building of the Vikings, the linen-making of the Huguenots, the words of Planter balladeers. How could we remove any one of these things from what we call our Irishness? Far from wanting to do so, we need to recover them so as to deepen our understanding.[60]

Clearly, then, Irish identity, Irishness and the Irish nation are concepts that have changed radically over the last two centuries, due to religious and political factors. There have been important differences not only in the religious composition of the perceived nation, but also in its political content with many Irish nationalists linking it to an independent state and many Irish unionists retaining a British context and dimension to their Irish nationality. At present Irish identity, in its political and cultural forms, is seen largely in nationalist terms, as linked to Irish nationalism and nationalist goals. It extends really only to the republic where the population is almost entirely catholic (protestants now comprising a mere 3%) and to the catholic and nationalist community of the north. A sense of Irishness is currently at an unparalleled low level among northern protestants and unionists. Today it is probably fair to say that the Irish nation and Irish nationality are defined in practice more exclusively than at any stage in the last two hundred years. The variety in views of Irish identity which used to exist has now largely disappeared. Nonetheless, some of the changes which have appeared recently may herald the beginning of a move to a broader interpretation once more.

7

HISTORICAL PERSPECTIVES IN AND ON
NORTHERN IRELAND

For anyone wishing to gain an understanding of present-day Northern Ireland, a knowledge of the history of the region is helpful. It is important not just to see things in their immediate context, but to appreciate the historical developments that have helped to create our contemporary world. Some of these developments we have shared with other places, while others are special, but rarely unique, to Northern Ireland. An appreciation of the history of our community can assist us in questioning many of the myths and half-truths in common circulation about our past. The aim of this essay is to describe the growth in historical research in and about Northern Ireland and to outline the work which has been done. Obviously this study cannot cover all the material on the subject, and so the information presented relates to the principal works on some of the leading subjects and themes of our history.

We will be concerned with the history of the six counties of Northern Ireland in the years 1921–68, but for the period before 1921 we will look at the history of the nine counties of Ulster right back to the beginning of the early modern period in the sixteenth century. It is important to remember, however, that our subject should not be seen in isolation. J.C. Beckett has stated: 'The history of Ulster is part of the history of Ireland, from which it cannot be wholly separated without distortion,' while at the same time he has acknowledged that the province has some distinctive characteristics, such as its connections with Scotland and its strong presbyterian influence.[1] The interaction of the various major cultures of the British Isles must be understood, as Hugh Kearney argues in his book *The British Isles: a history of four nations* (Cambridge, 1989). Likewise, the European context of many of the developments in Ulster cannot be ignored.

What are the themes and subjects of special interest in the history of Ulster? The conflict between unionism and nationalism is a leading theme in the politics of the province over the last century. In the social and economic area, the victory of tenants over landlords and the emergence of a rural economy based on small family-owned farms is significant. Religious division has been a major feature of society for many centuries. The relationship between religion and politics developed in important ways in the nineteenth and twentieth centuries. The expansion of an industrial base in eighteenth and nineteenth century Ulster has also been of great significance. Colonisation in early seventeenth century Ulster was of major importance. These are just some of the themes and subjects which historians have looked at in their studies of the history of Northern Ireland.

I

In the last quarter-century there has been a marked upsurge in the number of historical writings about Northern Ireland. This growth can be attributed partly to the new interest in our past caused by the recent 'troubles'. Partly, however, it must be seen as part of a process of a growing interest in the history of Ireland, north and south, which began in 1936 as a conscious movement to promote and develop Irish history, both in its methods and in its extent. Since that time this interest in our past has undergone important changes, as new areas of study came within its scope. Concern with political history has expanded to encompass concern with economic and social history, local history and, most recently, women's history. Besides these developments, debate has continued about the relevance and importance of our history, at popular and school level as well as in academic circles.

In February 1936 the Ulster Society for Irish Historical Studies was founded in Belfast, to be followed in November of the same year by the establishment of the Irish Historical Society in Dublin.[2] Their aim was to promote 'the advancement of Irish historical learning on scientific principles'. T.W. Moody, Belfast born history lecturer at The Queen's University of Belfast and later professor of history at Trinity College, Dublin, and Robin Dudley Edwards, lecturer and later professor of history at University College, Dublin, were the two leading figures in the appearance of the two societies, and they served also as the first editors of the new journal, *Irish Historical Studies*, founded in 1938 and owned jointly by the two societies.

Producing two issues a year, *Irish Historical Studies* set out 'to be of service to the specialist, the teacher, and the general reader who has an intelligent interest in the subject'. Since 1938 the journal has continued to produce important articles incorporating new research which has often led to reinterpretation of accepted views on particular topics. In addition it has printed material on research methods and documents. *Irish Historical Studies* remains the leading journal in the field of Irish history and continues to produce valuable material on the history of Northern Ireland as well as the rest of Ireland. Today historians would be more cautious about claiming to be totally 'scientific' in their research and writing. Nonetheless, the efforts of these pioneers of the 1930s, with their concern for a rigorous examination of original evidence, both primary and secondary, has led to a high degree of objectivity in the subject. J.J. Lee has commented:

> *Irish Historical Studies* took history out of politics. In its pages it is virtually impossible to identify authors as catholic or protestant, nationalist or unionist, southern or northern. In the context of the centuries-old polemical tradition, it would be difficult to exaggerate the significance of the achievement.[3]

In 1938 the Irish Committee of Historical Sciences was founded to represent historians from all over Ireland, to organise conferences, and to develop links with historians abroad. In the early 1950s the Irish Historical Students' Association was set up to run annual conferences for history students from Irish universities, north and south. Besides *Irish Historical Studies*, this co-operation among historians from both sides of the border is to be found in other history journals which have appeared since 1938. In 1970 the Economic and Social History Society of Ireland was founded, and four years later the society's journal, *Irish Economic and Social History*, was published for the first time. Two of the leading historians behind this development were Louis Cullen of Trinity College, Dublin, and Kenneth Connell of The Queen's University of Belfast. The following year saw the publication of the first issue of *Saothar: Journal of the Irish Labour History Society*. In 1992 *History Ireland* was established as a popular quarterly journal by a number of young historians at the Institute of Irish Studies at Queen's University Belfast, and published subsequently in Dublin. Its aim is to bring history to a wider audience, including the schools.

Another area of growth has been in local history, both as a subject and as a popular movement. In 1975 the Federation of Ulster Local Studies was established to create a central body for the growing number of local history societies from the nine counties of Ulster. It includes a wide range of county history societies, religious history organisations and local history or heritage bodies. Organisations such as the Belfast Natural History and Philosophical Society (founded 1821) and the Londonderry Naturalist Field Club (founded 1928) have long promoted local history studies among their interests. The Presbyterian Historical Society was founded in 1907, to be followed by the Methodist Historical Society in 1926: both were in practice province-wide rather than local organisations because of the structure and distribution of their respective denominations. After the Second World War, a number of societies dealing specifically with local history were established.

In 1946 the Donegal Historical Society, drawing on wide community support, was founded, and the following year saw the publication of the first volume of its journal, to be renamed *The Donegal Annual* in 1951. Catholic diocesan historical societies were formed for Clogher (1952), Armagh (1953) and Kilmore (1965), with their journals, *the Clogher Record*, *Seanchas Ardmhacha* and *Breifne*. Over the years they have covered a wide range of historical subjects for their areas, and their membership, especially for Clogher, is now much broader than when first established. In 1957 the Ulster Scot Historical Society was formed, and in 1975 its name was changed to the Ulster Historical Foundation: it has published a wide range of material on Ulster history and a journal called *Familia* with a special interest in family history. The Church of Ireland Historical Society was founded in Armagh in 1994. In recent decades there has been a rapid growth in the number of local history societies: in 1975 these groups totalled twenty but by 1995 the figure stood at seventy-five. There are four main local history societies for the four geographical parts of Belfast and numerous societies in every county of Ulster. These organisations usually have broad community support and often run well attended series of lectures. They include the Glens of Antrim Historical Society with its journal, *The Glynns*, the Lecale Historical Society with its journal *Lecale Miscellany* and the Ballinascreen Historical Society with its many published volumes of local material.

How do we explain this growth of interest in local history? In response to this question, Brian Turner has commented: 'A substantial part of this rise in interest can be attributed not just to the alienating effects of the modern world in general, but most particularly to some people's desire to understand how Ulster society has reached its present stage.'[4] There are also a number of more practical reasons. The last three decades have seen a growth in the role of the libraries, with considerable resources being given to local collections of material. The Public Record Office of Northern Ireland has played an important role in all this, gathering and making available a wide range of valuable local documents: its extensive publication programme has made much of this material easily accessible. The museums, along with the Workers' Education Association and Queen's extra-mural department, have contributed to the growth of local interest. The journal *Ulster Folklife* has been published in association with the Ulster Folk and Transport Museum since 1956. The appearance of several local publishers in recent decades has encouraged the publication of many useful volumes.

II

In addition to the valuable material produced by these societies through their publications, a large number of books have been written by individuals on the history of Northern Ireland. Some of this work is incorporated within general histories of Ireland which cover both north and south, while other writing has been more specifically centred on Northern Ireland. In the first category falls work by J.C. Beckett, lecturer and then professor of Irish history at Queen's, whose *Short history of Ireland* (London, 1952), ran into many editions, as did his later book, *The making of modern Ireland, 1603–1923* (London, 1966). T.W. Moody of Trinity College and F.X. Martin of University College, Dublin, were joint editors of a broad historical survey given as a series of Thomas Davis lectures on R.T.E., written by a representative selection of Irish historians and published under the title *The course of Irish history* (Cork, 1967), which became one of the most popular Irish general histories. Other similar works, covering different ranges of time, from academics such as J.J. Lee, R.F. Foster and F.S.L. Lyons, all include Northern Ireland in their texts. Another important work in this general category is the multi-volume *New history of Ireland*, published in Oxford in association with the Royal Irish Academy, Dublin.

Besides these general studies, it must be remembered that there are important volumes or articles on specific subjects or themes which include or relate to developments in the north. For example, W.E. Vaughan's writing on the land question in nineteenth century Ireland, especially his *Landlords and tenants in mid-Victorian Ireland, 1848–1903* (Oxford, 1994) and his pamphlet *Landlords and tenants in Ireland, 1848–1903* (Dundalk, 1984), is essential reading on the subject and con-

tains many Ulster examples. Understanding of northern
nationalism will be enhanced greatly by a study of D.G.
Boyce's *Nationalism in Ireland* (London, 1982; revised third
edition, 1995). Changes in nineteenth-century catholicism in
Ulster cannot be understood properly without a reading of
the work of Emmet Larkin, such as his article 'The devotional
revolution in Ireland, 1850–72' in *American Historical Review*,
lxxvii, no.3 (June, 1972), pp 625–52.

There are a number of general studies specifically on the
history of Northern Ireland. These volumes usually cover the
six counties of Northern Ireland from 1921 to the present,
but for the pre-1921 period they often cover all the nine
counties of Ulster. T.W. Moody and J.C. Beckett in the mid-
1950s organised a series of B.B.C. lectures, given by a wide
range of experts, which were then published as *Ulster since
1800: a political and economic survey* (London, 1955) and *Ulster
since 1800: a social survey* (London, 1957). These two books
were of seminal importance because they covered many subjects, including education, the growth of towns, industrial
conditions, the churches and the arts, and they provided a
starting-point for much of the more detailed work which has
followed. Other recent general studies include *Ulster: an illustrated history* (London, 1989), edited by Ciaran Brady, Mary
O'Dowd and Brian Walker, and *A history of Ulster* (Belfast,
1992) by Jonathan Bardon. Both these volumes deal with the
history of Ulster from early times to the present. The first is a
collection of essays organised chronologically, while the second is a general survey by one author.

Many aspects of the history of Northern Ireland have
received attention from historians in the period since 1936.
For those who wish to pursue particular aspects, whether in
the areas of modern political changes, eighteenth century
penal laws or seventeenth-century plantations, attention
should turn to the published lists of material relating to the
history of Ireland, produced by the Irish Committee of
Historical Sciences. It has published *Irish historiography,
1936–70* (Dublin, 1974), edited by T.W. Moody, and *Irish historiography, 1970–80* (Dublin, 1982), edited by J.J. Lee. As evidence of the growth of Irish history we may note that the

second volume, which covers only one decade, has nearly as many pages as the first volume, which ranges over nearly three and a half decades. Since 1980 a number of supplementary annual publications list new writing on Irish history.

A survey of these bibliographies reveals interesting changes in topics of research. Up to the mid-1970s it is fair to say that political subjects were of most concern. In the decade between the mid-1970s and the mid-1980s, as Ronan Fanning has pointed out, the most notable feature of Irish historiography has been the proliferation of publications in socio-economic history.[5] Since then there has been a growing interest in other subjects such as religious history, local history and women's studies, which has led to many valuable insights into the history of Northern Ireland. Having briefly explored the bibliographical background, we will now turn our attention to a survey of work on political history, followed by an examination of some of the other areas of interest.

III

A number of studies dealing with particular themes or subjects seek to give an interpretation of important aspects of Ulster's political history over a long period. David Miller in *Queen's rebels: Ulster loyalism in historical perspective* (Dublin, 1978) sees Ulster loyalist ideology as based on contractarian beliefs with roots in the seventeenth century. A.T.Q. Stewart in *The narrow ground: aspects of Ulster, 1609–1969* (London, 1977) views the conflict in Ulster as between two communities over the same territory for four centuries. A traditional Marxist view of the history of Ulster can be found in Liam de Paor's *Divided Ulster* (London, 1970; revised edition 1971). Ulster politics in the nineteenth and twentieth centuries are viewed in a comparative, worldwide perspective by Frank Wright in *Northern Ireland: a comparative analysis* (Dublin, 1987). A valuable discussion of these books and other publications as they contribute to the understanding of the political conflict in Northern Ireland can be found in John Whyte's *Interpreting Northern Ireland* (Oxford, 1990). Graham Walker is the author of a recent study of Ulster/Scottish relations, *Intimate strangers: political and cultural interaction between*

Scotland and Ulster in modern times (Edinburgh, 1995). I.S. Wood is editor of *Scotland and Ulster* (Edinburgh, 1994), which includes Ian Adamson's broad historical survey of the connections between the two, Linde Lunney's study of Scottish influences on eighteenth-century Ulster culture (looking especially at some of the weaver poets) and Graham Walker's examination of ideas of empire, religion and nationality in Scotland and Ulster before the first world war.

Various volumes provide a general survey of the history of Northern Ireland from 1921 to recent decades. These include Patrick Buckland's, *A history of Northern Ireland* (Dublin, 1981), David Harkness's *Northern Ireland since 1920* (London, 1983), and Michael Farrell's *Northern Ireland: the Orange State* (London, 1976; second edition, 1980). Paul Bew, Peter Gibbon and Henry Patterson are authors of *The state in Northern Ireland, 1921–72: political forces and social classes* (Manchester, 1979) which was subsequently updated and rewritten as *Northern Ireland, 1921–94: political forces and social classes* (London, 1995). The history of the unionist party in this period is covered in John Harbinson's *The Ulster unionist party, 1882–1973* (Belfast, 1973), while nationalism is dealt with by Eamon Phoenix in *Northern nationalism: nationalist parties, partition and the catholic minority in Northern Ireland, 1890–1940* (Belfast, 1994).

Some writers look at specific subjects and particular years since the establishment of Northern Ireland. Patrick Buckland is the author of *The factory of grievances: devolved government in Northern Ireland, 1921–39* (Dublin, 1979). Political developments in the 1920s and 1930s are also studied in Michael Farrell's *Arming the protestants: the formation of the Ulster special constabulary 1920–27* (Dingle, 1983) and Bryan Follis's *A state under siege: the establishment of Northern Ireland, 1920–25* (Oxford, 1995). Jennifer Todd's survey 'Unionist political thought, 1920–72' appears in George Boyce, Robert Eccleshall and Vincent Geoghegan (eds) *Political thought in Ireland since the seventeenth century* (London, 1993), pp 190–211. *Crying in the wilderness. Jack Sayers: a liberal editor in Ulster, 1939–69* (Belfast, 1995), edited by Andrew Gailey, is concerned primarily with Terence O'Neill's years as prime–minister.

Different dimensions of north and south relations are explored in *De Valera and the Ulster question, 1917–1973* (Oxford, 1982) by John Bowman, *Partition and the limits of Irish nationalism: an ideology under stress* (Dublin, 1987) by Clare O'Halloran, and *The widening gulf: northern attitudes to the independent Irish state, 1919–49* (Belfast, 1988) by Dennis Kennedy. David Harkness looks at north-south relations during the twentieth century in *Twentieth century Ireland: divided island* (London, 1995). Brian Barton is author of *Brookeborough: the making of a prime minister* (Belfast, 1988) and also *Northern Ireland in the second world war* (Belfast, 1995), which adds new material and perspectives to the official account of these years by J.W. Blake, published in Belfast in 1956 under the same title.

The political turmoil of the years 1912–14 is covered in A.T.Q. Stewart's *The Ulster crisis* (London, 1967). This period is also dealt with by Paul Bew in *Ideology and the Irish question: Ulster unionism and Irish nationalism* (Oxford, 1995). Philip Orr looks at the impact of the first world war on Ulster, in particular at the battle of the Somme in 1916, in his book *The road to the Somme: men of the Ulster division tell their story* (Belfast, 1987). Events leading to the partition of Ireland and the establishment of Northern Ireland are studied in Michael Laffan's *The partition of Ireland, 1911–25* (Dundalk, 1983). These events are also examined in *Nationalism and unionism: conflict in Ireland, 1885–1921* (Belfast, 1994), edited by Peter Collins. This volume includes chapters on the 1885–6 general elections, unionism, nationalism, labour and partition: many of these discuss developments in Ulster in detail. Republican reaction in Ulster in 1916 is described by F.X. Martin in 'Easter 1916: an inside report on Ulster' in *Clogher Record*, xii, no. 2 (1986) pp 192–208. The British and Irish Communist Organisation has been responsible for a number of historical writings including *Ulster as it is* (Belfast, 1973) and *The road to partition* (Belfast, 1974).

Ulster unionism of the late nineteenth and early twentieth centuries is studied by Patrick Buckland in *Irish unionism 2: Ulster unionism and the origins of Northern Ireland, 1886–1922* (Dublin, 1973). Alvin Jackson is the author of *The Ulster party:*

Irish unionists in the house of commons, 1884–1911 (Oxford, 1989), biographies of *Sir Edward Carson* (Dundalk, 1993) and *Colonel Edward Saunderson: land and loyalty in Victorian Ireland* (Oxford, 1995). A.T.Q. Stewart has written *Edward Carson* (Dublin, 1981). Alvin Jackson investigates the history of unionism in articles on the subject in the *Irish Review*, no. 7 (Autumn 1989), pp 58–65, and no. 8 (Spring 1990), pp 62–9. Biographies of two other figures with an Ulster connection in this period are *Roger Casement* (London, 1973) by Brian Inglis and *The scholarly revolutionary: Eoin MacNeill 1867–1945, and the making of the new Ireland* (Shannon, 1973) edited by F.X. Martin and F.J. Byrne. Patricia Jalland looks at the impact of the Ulster issue in British politics in the early twentieth-century in *The liberals and Ireland: the Ulster question in British politics to 1914* (Brighton, 1980).

Events in the critical years 1885–6 are studied in D.C. Savage's 'The origins of the Ulster unionist party, 1885–6 in *Irish Historical Studies*, xii no. 47, (March 1961), pp 185–208. *Ulster politics: the formative years, 1868–86* (Belfast, 1989) by B.M. Walker, looks at the changes of these years for all the parties in Ulster and describes the emergence of unionism and nationalism based on religious divisions, as well as analysing political developments from 1868 onwards. James Loughlin examines the impact of the issue of Ulster on national politics in his book *Gladstone, home rule and the Ulster question 1882–93* (Dublin, 1986). Alistair Cooke deals with connections between Ulster politicians and the conservative party in Great Britain in 'A conservative leader in Ulster: Sir Stafford Northcote's diary of a visit to the province, October 1883', in *Proceedings of the Royal Irish Academy*, lxxv, section C (September 1975). Tom Hennessey looks at unionist ideology at the end of the nineteenth century in 'Ulster unionist territorial and national identities: province, island, kingdom and empire' in *Irish Political Studies*, viii, (1993), pp 21–36. Gordon Lucy has written *The great convention: the Ulster unionist convention of 1892* (Lurgan, 1995).

The impact of the land question on Ulster politics and society is the subject of a number of studies. 'The agrarian opposition in Ulster politics, 1848–87' by Paul Bew and Frank

Wright and 'The land question and elections in Ulster, 1868–86' by B.M. Walker are to be found in Samuel Clark and J.S. Donnelly (eds), *Irish peasants: violence and political unrest, 1780–1914* (Manchester, 1983), pp 192–268. Robert Kirkpatrick is the author of 'Origins and development of the land war in mid-Ulster' in F.S.L. Lyons and R.A.J. Hawkins (eds), *Ireland under the union: varieties of tension: essays in honour of T.W. Moody* (Oxford, 1980), pp 201–35. Frank Thompson assesses the impact of the land question in Ulster at Westminster in the 1880s in 'Attitudes to reform: political parties in Ulster and the Irish land bill of 1881,' in *Irish Historical Studies*, xxiv, no. 95 (May 1985), pp 327–40. Home rule politics in Ulster in this period are examined by Jack Magee in 'The Monaghan election of 1883 and the "invasion of Ulster" in *Clogher Record,* viii, (1974), pp 147–67 and by Gerard Moran in 'The advance on the north: the difficulties of the home rule movement in south-east Ulster, 1870–83' in Raymond Gillespie and Harold O'Sullivan (eds), *The borderlands: essays on the history of Ulster-Leinster border* (Belfast, 1989), pp 129–42.

Events in late eighteenth-century Ulster have attracted much attention from historians. Most books on the United Irishmen contain considerable material on the north. Charles Dickson's *Revolt in the north: Antrim and Down in 1798* (Dublin, 1960) is specifically concerned with Ulster and includes important documents from various sources. Another pack of documents, entitled *The 1798 rebellion,* in the Public Record Office of Northern Ireland educational facsimile series, also contains useful original material. Mary McNeill's book, *The life and times of Mary Ann McCracken, 1770–1866: a Belfast panorama* (Dublin, 1960; reprint Belfast, 1988), is concerned with the subject's involvement not only in United Irish politics but also in many aspects of Belfast's cultural and social life. A.T.Q. Stewart examines the background to the United Irishmen in *A deeper silence: the hidden origins of the United Irishmen* (London, 1993), while he describes day-to-day events of the 1798 rising in Ulster in *summer soldiers: the 1798 rebellion in Antrim and Down* (Belfast, 1995). *The United Irishmen: republicanism, radicalism and rebel-*

lion (Dublin, 1993), edited by David Dickson, Dáire Keogh and Kevin Whelan, includes various chapters on Ulster. In this volume Peter Tesch has written on presbyterian radicalism, Ian McBride on William Drennan and the dissenting tradition, W.H. Crawford on the Belfast middle classes in the late eighteenth century. N.J. Curtin on the United Irish organisation in Ulster in 1795–8, Marianne Elliott on the defenders in Ulster and Allan Blackstock on the social and political implications of the raising of the yeomanry in Ulster in 1796–8.

Several works deal with the background to the founding of the Orange Order. David Miller is author of 'The Armagh troubles, 1784–95' in Samuel Clark and J.S. Donnelly (eds) *Irish peasants: violence and political unrest, 1780–1914* (Manchester, 1983), pp 155–91 and editor of *Peep o'day Boys and Defenders: selected documents on the county Armagh disturbances, 1784–96* (Belfast, 1990). Another volume which looks at the origins of the Orange Order is *The formation of the Orange Order 1795–98: the edited papers of Colonel William Blacker and Colonel R.H. Wallace.* (Belfast, 1994). The political position of Ulster presbyterians in the eighteenth and late seventeenth-centuries is examined in J.C. Beckett's *Protestant dissent in Ireland, 1687–1780* (London, 1948). Changes affecting the catholic community in Ulster are investigated by W.H. Crawford in 'The Ulster Irish in the eighteenth-century' in *Ulster Folklife*, xxviii, (1982), pp 24–32 and by Tomás Ó Fiaich in three articles entitled 'The O'Neills of the Fews' in *Seanchas Ardmhacha*, vii, no. 1 (1973), pp 1–64, vii, no. 2 (1974), pp 263–315, and viii, no.2 (1977) pp 386–413. Agrarian conflict in Ulster in the 1770s and 1780s is the subject of a study by J.S. Donnelly, 'Hearts of Oak, Hearts of Steel' in *Studia Hibernica*, xxi, 1981, pp 7–73.

The siege of Derry has been covered in J.G. Simms's *The siege of Derry* (Dublin, 1966) and Patrick Macrory's *The siege of Derry* (London, 1980). The impact of the Battle of the Boyne on the history of Ulster, Ireland and Europe is dealt with by Ian Adamson in *1690, William and the Boyne* (Belfast, 1995) and in W.A. Maguire (ed.), *Kings in conflict: the revolutionary war in Ireland and its aftermath* (Belfast, 1990). Chapters in this latter book examine events of 1689–91, both within Ireland and in the European context, and study the consequences of the outcome of the battle in matters such as the future land settlement and the penal laws. The activities of a legendary outlaw and former Gaelic landowner in Ulster in the 1670s are examined by T.W. Moody in 'Redmond O'Hanlon' in *Proceedings and reports of the Belfast Natural History and Philosophical Society*, 2nd series, i, (1937), pp 17–33. David Stevenson, in *Scottish covenanters and Irish confederates* (Belfast, 1981) looks at Scottish-Irish relations in the mid-seventeenth century, with particular reference to Ulster. Two leading catholic ecclesiastical figures of the seventeenth century are covered by Tomás Ó Fiaich in 'The appointment of Blessed Oliver Plunkett to Armagh' in *Irish Theological Quarterly*, xxv (1958), pp 144–53, and 'Edmund O'Reilly, archbishop of Armagh, 1657–69' in Franciscan Fathers (eds), *Father Luke Wadding* (Dublin, 1957), pp 171–228.

Considerable attention has been paid to political events in Ulster in the early decades of the seventeenth century. The arrival of large numbers of Scots in various parts of the province has been described in Michael Perceval-Maxwell's *The Scottish migration to Ulster in the reign of James I* (London, 1973). Raymond Gillespie looks at the impact of new arrivals, mainly Scottish, in Cos Down and Antrim in his *Colonial Ulster: the settlement of east Ulster, 1600–41* (Cork, 1985). Developments in another county are the subject of T.W. Moody's pioneering study, *The Londonderry plantation, 1609–41: the city of London and the plantation of Ulster* (Belfast, 1939). R.J. Hunter is author of 'English undertakers in the plantation of Ulster' in *Breifne*, iv (1973–5), pp 471–500.

Gaelic response to the changes in early seventeenth-century Ulster is examined in a number of studies. The departure of the leading Ulster Gaelic chieftains in 1607 is investigated in N.P. Canny's 'The flight of the earls' in *Irish Historical Studies*, xvii, no.67 (March, 1971), pp 380–99, and in John McCavitt's 'The flight of the earls, 1607' in *Irish Historical Studies*, xxix, no.114 (November 1994), pp 159–73. T.W. Moody was author of 'The treatment of the native population under the scheme for the plantation of Ulster' in *Irish*

Historical Studies i, no.1 (March 1938). In *Breifne,* xxiii (1985), pp 233–62, Ciaran Brady has written on 'The O'Reillys of east Breifne and the problems of surrender and regrant,' while in *Irish Geography,* xiv, (1981), pp 1–26, P.J. Duffy has looked at 'The territorial organisation of Gaelic ownership and its transformation in Co. Monaghan, 1591–1640'. Raymond Gillespie examines the reaction of some prominent Gaelic figures in *Conspiracy: Ulster plots and plotters in 1615* (Belfast, 1987). The career of a leading Gaelic chieftain is examined in Micheline Kerney Walsh's *Destruction by peace: Hugh O'Neill after Kinsale: Glanconcadhain, 1602 – Rome 1616* (Armagh, 1986).

Events in Ulster during the rising of 1641 are dealt with extensively in *Ulster 1641: aspects of the rising* (Belfast, 1993), edited by Brian MacCuarta. Articles in the volume include: the political background to the Ulster plantation, 1607–20, by John McCavitt; protestantism in Ulster, 1610–41, by Phil Kilroy; Ulster exiles in Europe, 1605–41 by Gráinne Henry; the native Ulster *mentalité* as revealed in Gaelic sources, 1600–50, by Michelle O Riordan; destabilising Ulster, 1641–2, by Raymond Gillespie; violence in County Armagh, 1641, by Hilary Simms. Other chapters cover Ulster in 1641 in the context of political developments in the three kingdoms, by Michael Perceval-Maxwell; the 1641 rebellion and anti-popery in Ireland, by Aidan Clarke; 1641 and the quest for catholic emancipation, 1691–1829 by Jacqueline Hill, and a bibliographical essay on 1641 by Toby Barnard.

Information on the state of Ulster at the end of the sixteenth century can be found in G.A. Hayes-McCoy's *Ulster and other Irish maps c. 1600* (Dublin, 1964). Changes in Gaelic society and leadership are examined in 'Hugh O'Neill, earl of Tyrone, and the changing face of Gaelic Ulster,' in *Studia Hibernica,* x, (1970), pp 7–35, by N.P.Canny, and, also in 'The end of Gaelic Ulster: a thematic interpretation of events between 1574 and 1610' in *Irish Historical Studies,* xxvi, no.191, (May, 1988), pp 8–32, and 'Hugh O'Neill and the Nine Years War in Tudor Ireland' in *Historical Journal,* xxxvi, no. 1, (1993) pp 21–37, both by Hiram Morgan who is also the author of *Tyrone's rebellion, the outbreak of the Nine Years War in*

Tudor Ireland (London, 1993). For information on Ulster at the beginning of the early modern period, attention should be paid to Aubrey Gwynn's *The medieval province of Armagh, 1470–1545* (Dundalk, 1946) and D.B. Quinn's 'Ulster, 1460–1550' *in Proceedings of the Belfast Naturalist History and Philosophical Society*, 1933–4, pp 56–78 (reprinted 1935).

IV

The economic and social history of Northern Ireland has been the subject of many studies over recent decades. An important pioneer was E.R.R. Green with his first book, *The Lagan valley, 1800–50* (London, 1949), which examined the origins of industrialisation in north-east Ulster, and later studies which included *The industrial archaeology of County Down* (Belfast, 1963). W.A. McCutcheon is author of *The industrial archaeology of Northern Ireland* (Belfast, 1980) while H.D. Gribbon wrote *The history of water power in Ulster* (Newton Abbot, 1969), and W.E. Coe produced *The engineering industries of the north of Ireland* (Newton Abbot, 1969). Belfast shipbuilding has been investigated in an article 'Shipbuilding in Belfast, 1861–1986' by Frank Geary and D.S. Johnson in *Irish Economic and Social History*, xvi (1989), pp 42–64, and in a book *Shipbuilders to the world: 125 years of Harland and Wolff, Belfast, 1861–1986* (Belfast, 1986) by Michael Moss and J.R. Hume.

Industry is one of a number of topics dealt with in *An economic history of Ulster, 1820–1939* (Manchester, 1985), edited by Liam Kennedy and Philip Ollerenshaw. This volume contains essays on the rural economy, 1820–1914, by Liam Kennedy; industry, 1820–1914, by Philip Ollerenshaw; transport, 1820–1914 by W.A. McCutcheon; population change and urbanisation 1821–1911, by L.A. Clarkson; and industrial labour and the labour movement, 1820–1914 by Henry Patterson. In the same book D.S. Johnson looks at the Northern Ireland economy, 1914–39, while John Othick gives a comparative perspective on the economic history of Ulster. Philip Ollerenshaw is also the author of *The Belfast banks, 1825–1914* (Manchester, 1987) and 'Textiles and regional economic decline: Northern Ireland, 1914–70' in Colin

Holmes and Alan Booth (eds), *Economy and society: European industrialisation and its social consequences* (Leicester, 1991), pp 58–83.

The land question was a matter of central importance in nineteenth century Ulster, as elsewhere in Ireland. W.E. Vaughan looks at issues of evictions and landlord power in his case study of a Donegal landlord –*Sin, sheep and Scotsmen: John George Adair and the Derryveagh evictions, 1861* (Belfast, 1983). Landlord-tenant relations in the first half of the nineteenth century are investigated in W.A. Maguire's *The Downshire estates in Ulster, 1801–45* (Oxford, 1972) and in a *General report on the Gosford estates in County Armagh 1821 by William Greig* (Belfast, 1976), edited by W.H. Crawford.

A number of studies of the effects of the Great Famine in Ulster have helped to illustrate the local impact of this countrywide disaster. James Grant has written on 'Aspects of the Great Famine in County Armagh' in *Seanchas Ardmhacha*, (1977), and on 'The Great Famine and the poor law in Ulster: the rate-in-aid issue of 1849' in *Irish Historical Studies*, xxvii, no. 105 (May 1990), pp 30–47. Margaret Quinn is the author of 'Enniskillen Poor Law Union, 1840–9' in *Clogher Record*, vii, no. 3 (1971–3). The Public Record Office of Northern Ireland, in a collection of documents, entitled *The Great Famine* and published in their series of educational facsimiles, have reproduced considerable material relating to Ulster. A unique insight into pre-famine Ulster is given in the ordnance survey parish memoirs, written in the 1830s, and published in the 1990s in Belfast in a special 41 volume series under the editorship of Angélique Day and Patrick McWilliams.

The development of the linen industry in eighteenth and early nineteenth-century Ulster is examined by W.H. Crawford in *The handloom weavers and the Ulster linen industry* (Belfast, 1994) and in 'The evolution of the linen trade in Ulster before industrialisation' in *Irish Economic and Social History*, xv (1988), pp 32–53. The same author has written 'Economy and society in South Ulster in the eighteenth century' in *Clogher Record*, viii, no.3 (1975), pp 241–58. For documentary information covering social life in Ulster in the eighteenth century attention should be paid to the collection of documents from the Public Record Office of Northern Ireland edited by W.H. Crawford and Brian Trainor, *Aspects of Irish social history, 1750–1800* (Belfast, 1969).

Emigration from eighteenth century Ulster has been investigated by R.J. Dickson in *Ulster emigration to colonial America, 1718–75* (London, 1968; reprint Belfast, 1988). The fate of the Ulster emigrants to America is the subject of a number of essays in E.R.R. Green's *Essays in Scotch-Irish history* (London, 1969; reprint Belfast, 1992). A.S. Link examines the presbyterian Ulster/Scottish background of Woodrow Wilson; M.A. Jones gives an overview of Ulster emigration, 1783–1815; E.E. Evans looks at the cultural adaptation of the Scotch-Irish in America; and E.R.R. Green studies a number of Ulster emigrants' letters.

Changes to the economy and society of Ulster in the seventeenth century, especially in the first half, are the subject of several studies. The effects of the plantation on the landscape are examined by Philip Robinson in *The plantation of Ulster: British settlement in an Irish landscape, 1600–70* (Dublin, 1984). J.S. Curl looks at the impact of the plantation and subsequent developments on the landscape and architecture of one county in *The Londonderry plantation, 1609–1914* (Chichester, 1986). R.J. Hunter is the author of 'Ulster plantation towns' in D.W. Harkness and Mary O'Dowd (eds) *The town in Ireland* (Belfast, 1981), pp 55–80, while Raymond Gillespie has written 'The evolution of an Ulster urban network, 1600–41' in *Irish Historical Studies*, xxiv, (1984–5), pp 15–29.

V

New interest in urban history has led to the publication of a number of important books on the history of Belfast. In 1967 the B.B.C. published a series of radio lectures on Belfast, edited by J.C. Beckett and R.E. Glasscock. Entitled *Belfast: the origins and growth of an industrial city*, the book looked at a wide range of subjects on the history of Belfast, depicting its transformation from a town of 20,000 people in 1800 to a city with a population of over a third of a million one century later. The year 1978 saw the publication of two more histories

of Belfast: *Belfast: the making of the city* (Belfast), with an introduction by J.C. Beckett was another collection of essays, covering subjects such as community relations and popular
entertainment in nineteenth century Belfast, while *Belfast: an
illustrated history* (Belfast) was a full-length survey by Jonathan
Bardon. W.A. Maguire is the author of *Belfast* (Keele, 1993),
one of a series of historic surveys of towns and cities in the
British Isles. Maurice Goldring examines *Belfast: from loyalty to
rebellion* (London, 1991) in another series which looks at the
social and cultural character of European cities. C.E.B. Brett
is author of *Buildings of Belfast, 1700–1914* (London, 1967;
reprint Belfast, 1986)

A number of books have looked at specific periods or subjects in the history of Belfast. Andrew Boyd's *Holy war in
Belfast* (Tralee, 1969) investigated riots in Belfast in Belfast
over the previous century. Social tensions in the city were
investigated in Paddy Devlin's *Yes, we have no bananas: outdoor
relief in Belfast, 1920–39* (Belfast, 1981) and Sybil Gribbon's
Edwardian Belfast: a social profile (Belfast, 1982). A.C. Hepburn
looks at 'Belfast, 1871–1911: work, class and religion' in *Irish
Economic and Social History*, x (1983), pp 33–50. Belfast politics
from the early seventeenth century until the 1960s are investigated in *Belfast: approach to crisis, a study of Belfast politics*
(Belfast, 1973) by Ian Budge and Cornelius O'Leary.

Different aspects of Belfast political and social life were
studied in *Class conflict and sectarianism: the protestant working
class and the Belfast labour movement* (Belfast, 1980) by Henry
Patterson; *City in revolt: James Larkin and the Belfast dock strike of
1907* (Belfast, 1985) by John Gray; *The politics of frustration:
Harry Midgley and the failure of labour in Northern Ireland*
(Manchester, 1985) by Graham Walker; and *Labour and parti-
tion: the Belfast working class 1905–23* (London, 1991) by
Austen Morgan. Belfast politics are a major concern of Peter
Gibbon's *The origins of Ulster* unionism (Manchester, 1975).
The impact of the 1941 blitz on Belfast is examined by Brian
Barton in *The Blitz: Belfast in the war years* (Belfast, 1989).
Alison Jordan was author of *Who cared? Charity in Victorian and
Edwardian Belfast* (Belfast, 1993), while Eric Gallagher wrote
At points of need: the story of Belfast Central Mission, 1889–1989

(Belfast, 1989). Other urban studies include Tony Canavan's *Frontier town: an illustrated history of Newry* (Belfast, 1989) and Brian Lacy's *Siege city: the story of Derry and Londonderry* (Belfast, 1990).

VI

Religious history has attracted growing attention in recent years. Because most of the churches are organised on an island basis, much of the literature covers all of Ireland, especially in the cases of the catholic church and Church of Ireland. But there are a number of valuable northern studies. Biographies of important church figures include *Henry Cooke* (Belfast, 1981) by R.G.F. Holmes and *Patrick Dorrian: bishop of Down and Connor 1865–85* (Dublin, 1987) and *William Crolly: archbishop of Armagh 1835–49* (Dublin, 1994) both by Ambrose Macaulay. Sean Connolly is the author of 'Catholicism in Ulster, 1800–50' in Peter Roebuck (ed.) *Plantation to partition: essays in Ulster history in honour of J.L. McCracken* (Belfast, 1981), pp 157–71, while Oliver Rafferty is the author of the larger study *Catholicism in Ulster, 1603–1983* (Dublin, 1994). The role of the catholic church in Northern Ireland in the early twentieth century is examined in *The catholic church and the foundation of the Northern Irish state* (Cork, 1993) by Mary Harris.

Special aspects of Ulster presbyterianism are covered by David Miller, 'Presbyterianism and "modernisation" in Ulster' in *Past and Present*, no. 80, (1978), pp 66–90, by Richard McMinn, 'Presbyterianism and politics in Ulster, 1871–1906' in *Studia Hibernica*, xx (1981), pp 127–46; and by R.G.F. Holmes, 'Ulster presbyterianism and Irish nationalism' in S. Mews (ed.) *Religion and national identity : studies in church history* (Oxford, 1982), pp 535–48. R.G.F. Holmes is also author of *Our Irish presbyterian heritage* (Belfast, 1985), which is mainly concerned with Ulster presbyterians while Peter Brooke has written *Ulster presbyterianism: the historical perspective, 1610–1970* (Dublin, 1987). Methodism in Ulster is covered in Frederick Jeffery's *Irish methodism* (Belfast, 1964) and David Hempton's 'Methodism in Irish society, 1770–1830' in *Transactions of the Royal Historical Society*, 5th series, 36 (1986), pp 117–42. Material on the Church of Ireland in Ulster can be found in Michael Hurley's *Irish Anglicanism, 1869–1969* (Dublin, 1970), especially in the chapter 'Aspects of the northern situation' by David Kennedy, and also in *As by law established: the Church of Ireland since the reformation* (Dublin, 1995), edited by Alan Ford, James McGuire and Kenneth Milne.

The social history of popular protestantism is examined by David Hempton and Myrtle Hill in *Evangelical protestantism in Ulster Society, 1740–1890* (London, 1992). The historical role of all denominations in northern politics and society is investigated by John Fulton in *The tragedy of belief: division, politics and religion in Ireland* (Oxford, 1991). Church relations in the twentieth century are studied by Ian Ellis in *Vision and reality: a survey of twentieth century Irish inter-church relations.* M.W. Dewar, John Brown and S.E. Long are authors of *Orangeism: a new historical appreciation* (Belfast, 1967). A prominent nineteenth-century Orangeman is examined by Aiken McClelland in *William Johnston of Ballykilbeg* (Belfast, 1990).

Work on the cultural history of Ulster has produced some important studies. J.W. Foster has investigated the role of the Belfast Natural History and Philosophical Society and the Belfast Naturalists' Field Club in 'Natural history, science and Irish culture' in Gerald Dawe and J.W. Foster (eds) *The poet's place: Ulster literature and society* (Belfast, 1991), pp 119–29. The contribution of the former organisation to the development of the Ulster Museum is discussed by Noel Nesbitt, *A museum in Belfast* (Belfast, 1980). J.R.R. Adams has investigated the printed material read by the ordinary people of Ulster in the eighteenth and nineteenth century in his book, *The printed word and the common man: popular culture in Ulster, 1700–1900* (Belfast, 1987). John Killen is the author of *A history of the Linen Hall Library, 1788–1988* (Belfast, 1990). The role of the B.B.C. in the local context has been discussed by Rex Cathcart in *The most contrary region: the B.B.C. in Northern Ireland, 1924–1984* (Belfast, 1984). Two books which examine the history of the local press in its social and political setting are *A century of northern life: the Irish News and 100 years of Ulster history* (Belfast, 1995), edited by Eamon Phoenix, and *The*

Tele: a history of the Belfast Telegraph (Belfast, 1995) by Malcolm Brodie.

Important insights into Ulster cultural history are to be found in John Hewitt's study of the weaver poets of the early nineteenth-century, *Rhyming weavers and other country poets of Antrim and Down* (Belfast, 1974). D.H. Akenson and W.H. Crawford set one such poet in his social context in *Local poets and social history: James Orr, bard of Ballycarry* (Belfast, 1977). Other interesting views of the historical value of this material can be found in Jane Gray's 'Folk poetry and working-class identity in Ulster: an analysis of James Orr's "The penitent" ' in *Journal of Historical Sociology*, vi, no.3 (September, 1993), pp 249–75 and in Ivan Herbison's 'A sense of place: landscape and locality in the work of the rhyming weavers' in Gerald Dawe and J.W. Foster (eds) *The poet's place: Ulster literature and society* (Belfast, 1991), pp 63–76. As regards the history of the Irish language in Ulster, attention must be paid to *Hidden Ulster: protestants and the Irish language* (Belfast, 1995, first published 1973) by Padraig Ó Snodaigh and *Irish in County Down since 1750* by Ciarán Ó Duibhín (Downpatrick, 1991). Seventeenth and eighteenth century poets writing in Irish in south Ulster are discussed by Tomás Ó Fiaich in 'The political background of the Ulster poets' in *Léachtaí Cholm Chille*, i (1970), pp 23–33.

The development of education at different levels has received the attention of a number of historians. D.H. Akenson has examined changes in the school system in Northern Ireland since 1920 in *Education and enmity: the control of schooling in Northern Ireland, 1920–50* (Newton Abbot, 1973). Sean Farren has compared educational developments, north and south, in their political context in *The politics of Irish education* (Belfast, 1995). Among school histories, mention must be made of A.T.Q. Stewart's *Belfast Royal Academy: the first century, 1785–1885* (Belfast, 1985), John Jamieson's, *The history of the Royal Belfast Academical Institution, 1810–1960* (Belfast, 1959), Keith Haines's *Neither rogues nor fools: a history of Campbell College and Campbellians* (Belfast, 1993) and the collection of essays in *St Malachy's College, a sesquicentennial history* (Belfast, 1982). T.W. Moody and J.C.

Beckett were joint authors of the two volumed, *Queen's Belfast, 1845–1949: the history of a university* (London, 1959). Alf McCleary and B.M Walker wrote *Degrees of excellence: the story of Queen's, Belfast, 1845–1995* (Belfast, 1994).

The area of local studies has been enriched by the publication of a host of valuable writings in the last few decades. Local journals contain an enormous range of useful articles which contribute significantly to the larger historical picture.[6] It is possible here only to mention a few useful books on the subject. Two county histories of special note are *The Fermanagh story* (Enniskillen, 1969) and *The Monaghan story* (Enniskillen, 1980) by Peadar Livingstone. Desmond Murphy has studied politics and society in the north-west of the province in *Derry, Donegal and modern Ulster, 1790–1921* (Derry, 1981). D.H. Akenson has looked at a much smaller area in the east in the same period, *Between two revolutions: Islandmagee, County Antrim, 1798–1920* (Ontario, 1979). L.A. Clarkson and Margaret Crawford have investigated the lifestyle and activities of an eighteenth-century Armagh family in *Ways to wealth: the Cust family of eighteenth century Armagh* (Belfast, 1985). A County Antrim farm and family in the nineteenth and early twentieth-centuries are the subject of a study by B.M. Walker in *Sentry Hill: an Ulster farm and family* (Belfast, 1984; new edition, 1994). *Donegal: history and society* (Dublin, 1995), edited by Mary Dunlevy, William Nolan and Liam Ronayne is the first Ulster county to be covered in this Ireland-wide series of county histories. Another Ulster county history is *Cavan: essays on the history of an Irish county* (Dublin, 1995), edited by Raymond Gillespie.

Photographic history has been the subject of much research since the late 1960s. The first person in Northern Ireland to use early photographs effectively to illuminate our history was Noel Nesbitt in *The changing face of Belfast* (Belfast, 1969). This was followed by two photographic books edited by B.M. Walker: the first was *Faces of the past: a photographic and literary picture of Ulster life* (Belfast, 1974), which presented a wide range of photographic images; the second was *Shadows on glass: a portfolio of early Ulster photography* (Belfast, 1976), which looked at life in Ulster between the 1860s and 1920s through the work of thirteen different photographers. Since 1976 there have been a number of studies of the work of particular photographers, including *Ireland's eye: the photography of R.J. Welch* (Belfast, 1977), edited by Brian Turner and E.E.Evans, *Caught in time, the photographs of Alexander Hogg of Belfast, 1870–1939* (Belfast, 1986) edited by W.A. Maguire, and *The way we were, historic Armagh photographs from the Allison collection* (Belfast, 1993), edited by Roger Weatherup and Desmond Fizgerald. A selection of photographs from a newspaper file was presented by David Bigger and Terence McDonald in their book *In sunshine or in shadow, photographs from the Derry Standard, 1928–39* (Belfast, 1990).

Biographies and autobiographies can provide valuable insight into our history. In addition to those already mentioned in this text under specific subject areas, there are a number of volumes in this category which should be listed. Kate Newmann's *Dictionary of Ulster biography* (Belfast, 1993) gives brief biographical entries on nearly 2000 persons from Ulster. *Nine Ulster lives* (Belfast, 1992), edited by Gerard O'Brien and Peter Roebuck, has chapters on Ernest Walton by Brian Cathcart, Claude Auchinleck by T.G. Fraser, Helen Waddell by Felicitas Corrigan, John Lavery by Kenneth McConkey, Charles Gavan Duffy by Gerard O'Brien, John Dunlop by Roy McCaughey, William Paterson by Steve Ickringill, John Abernethy by A. Godfrey Brown and Owen Roe O'Neill by Raymond Gillespie. Séan McMahon and Art Byrne are the editors of *Great northerners* (Dublin, 1991). Sophia King has edited the anthology *Between history and hope: first-hand accounts of Ulster life, 1901–94* (Belfast, 1996). Recently we have seen the publication of *The autobiography of Thomas Witherow 1824–1890* (Ballinascreen, 1990) and *A life in linenopolis: the memoirs of William Topping, Belfast damask weaver, 1903–56* (Belfast, 1992).

Women's history has been the subject of much research in recent years. An important pioneer of the subject was Alison Jordan, author of *Margaret Byers: pioneer of women's education and founder of Victoria College, Belfast* (Belfast, 1991). Alison Jordan was also the contributor of an article entitled 'Opening the gates of learning: the Belfast Ladies' Institute,

1867–97' in a volume, *Coming into the light: the work, politics and religion of women in Ulster, 1840–1940* (Belfast, 1994), edited by Janice Holmes and Diane Urquhart. Chapters include essays on religion: 'The world turned upside down: women in the Ulster revival of 1859' by Janice Holmes, 'The cursed cup hath cast her down: constructions of female piety in Ulster evangelical temperance literature, 1863–1914' by A.E. Brozyna; and 'The genesis of convent foundations and their institutions in Ulster, 1840–1920' by Marie O'Connell. In the section on politics, Brigitte Anton has written 'Northern voices: Ulsterwomen in the Young Ireland movement' and Diane Urquhart is author of ' "The female of the species is deadlier than the male?" The Ulster Women's Unionist Council, 1911–40', while Margaret Neill contributed 'Homeworkers in Ulster, 1850–1911.'

Clearly, then, recent decades have witnessed the publication of much valuable material on the history of Northern Ireland. It has only been possible to survey some of the areas covered in this ongoing research. Other areas in which important work has been done but which are not covered here include the histories of medicine, the arts, material culture, the military and architecture. Developments in oral history and folklore have not been discussed. Nonetheless, the books and articles covered in this chapter serve to illustrate the intense and thorough investigation of our history which is taking place. The origins of this new work lie in the 1930s, but efforts of the last three decades have transformed the sheer volume of the ongoing research. New areas of study continue to be pursued. Professor Marianne Elliott has stated, 'Irish history has been misinterpreted by all sides and has been used as a weapon to support various polemical stances.' She concludes: 'Real knowledge of what happened will show how selective our history has been and that the stereotypical views that people have are incorrect.'[7]

FINAL OBSERVATIONS

In his 1996 St Patrick's Day message President Clinton reiterated his support for peace in Northern Ireland and stated that 'those who are blinded by the hatreds of the past' must not be allowed to destroy the peace process. In his speech to the Irish houses of parliament in December 1995 he referred to his trip to Belfast where he saw optimism 'in the face of two communities, divided by bitter history.'[1] Eight months earlier Sir Patrick Mayhew described the theme from another speech of President Clinton's as 'let us turn the key upon history and go forward into new uplands free from the burdens of the history of the past.'[2] Recent editorials in London newspapers reflect this view of the importance of history in Ireland. On 3 June 1995, following protests over a royal visit to Dublin, an editorial in the *Daily Telegraph* declared: 'history in Ireland takes a long time to work itself out.' On 2 December 1995, in response to the continuation of violence in spite of the cease-fire, an editorial in the *Times* warned that 'shades of the past lurk angrily in the wings, ready to claim the province once more.' On 3 December 1995, after the Irish divorce referendum and President Clinton's visit, the *Sunday Times* declared: 'For centuries a cloistered corner of Europe, apparently immune to social and political developments elsewhere, both the north and south of the island turned their backs on the past.' This belief in the relevance of the past in Ireland is shared by many observers.

In this book, however, it has been argued that Ireland is not in fact linked in a special way to the past or history. The conflict within Northern Ireland and between north and south is primarily to do with contemporary divisions over religion and nationalism. In the chapter on the 1885 and 1886 general elections we saw how in the last decades of the nineteenth century, problems over nationalism and religion emerged as key issues for modern twentieth century Ireland, north and south. Events of 1912–23 would affect the constitutional and territorial shape of the new Northern Ireland, but the basic character of its internal divisions was established at these crucial earlier elections. In chapter three attention focused on the continued reality of religious division in the twentieth century.

A major point to emerge is that Ireland is not unique in a European context. Political conflict over both nationalism and religion has been apparent in many parts of modern Europe, and this period of the late nineteenth and early twentieth centuries was crucial for its emergence. What is special about Ireland is the particular combination of these important divisions. The appearance of the confrontation in Ireland in 1885–6, however, was not to do with a unique history but with other contemporary key factors such as the political skills and vision (or lack of vision) of the party leaders and organisers. Like elsewhere, the earlier history of Ireland cannot be ignored but it is this key formative period which sets the basic scene for the politics of modern-day Ireland.

Why do outside observers not understand this and why are they so keen on an historical interpretation which sees the conflict as a unique and 'age-old' one? At a conference in Washington in 1989 on the problems of Northern Ireland, Lord Armstrong, secretary of the cabinet and head of the home civil service in the U.K. in the 1980s, suggested that 'the English are not really able to understand in others what they lack in themselves', and because they have little sense of ethnicity they cannot understand problems over this matter in

Ireland.[3] In the 1920s, in his book *Ulster's stand for union,*
Ronald McNeill (later Lord Cushendun) attributed the
English failure to understand religious feeling in Ireland to
the fact that they had forgotten that their own recent history
included religious conflict (such as the anti-catholic riots of
the early 1850s) and that they knew little about contemporary
Europe where religion remained a key political issue (such as
in France in the early 1920s with deep rivalry between clerical
and anticlerical forces).[4] McNeill's comments are still true
today. For the vast majority of people in the Anglo-American
world in which we live there is no understanding of the problems over religion or nationalism, because they have neither
experienced these divisions personally nor understood them
elsewhere. For these people, to blame the conflict in Ireland
on history seems a reasonable explanation.

There is another good reason, of course, why outside
observers think that the past is very important in Ireland.
People in Ireland not only believe it themselves but their
actions are greatly influenced by this belief. The recent
report of the international body on decommissioning of
paramilitary weapons, chaired by Senator George Mitchell,
declared that: 'common to many of our meetings were arguments, steeped in history, as to why the other side cannot be
trusted.' It noted that: 'A resolution of the decommissioning
issue - or any other issue will not be found if the parties resort
to their vast inventories of historical recrimination.'[5] Conor
Cruise O'Brien has talked of 'ancestral voices' affecting
actions while J. Bowyer Bell has written about 'history's tune'
influencing people.[6] In chapter four we examined the frequent reference to the past in Ireland and sought to describe
its impact in a range of areas. President Clinton and others
are correct in a sense when they talk of the influence of the
past and history, but it must be realised that it is very often the
myths of the past which affect matters and which people
believe to be important.

In chapter one we looked at how unionists developed their
sense of history and how this came to incorporate a number
of myths. Some aspects of their view of the past were historically accurate while others were selective or inaccurate. This

sense of history developed over a period of time and only
became meaningful to the majority of that community at the
end of the nineteenth century. In response to the real
conflict which emerged in Ireland at this time, unionists
established an historical view, incorporating various myths
and creating traditions. The nationalist experience was the
same: they also developed a sense of history which was meaningful to their nineteenth century experiences. These new
views of the past fitted well the political and religious confrontation which emerged in this period. Such historical
views have remained at the heart of political and social dialogue in Ireland with considerable consequences for both
parts of the island. The strength and value for communities
in many of the traditions involved in these ideas of history
must be acknowledged, but it would be wrong to accept them
uncritically.

These historical views, if taken at full face value, can create a
number of serious difficulties. First, they give a selective,
incomplete and sometimes inaccurate picture to a community
of its own history. Secondly, they obscure the real nature of the
problem which is conflict over religion and nationalism. Other
European countries have faced these vexed questions and have
found ways to cope with them better than has been the case in
Ireland. Fascination with a supposedly unique history has
obscured both the reality and the opportunity to effectively
confront the problem. The significance of the role of both people and leaders in bringing about the new arrangements of
1885–6, as well as their continued involvement in their maintenance, emphasises the responsibility of people and leaders
today. The third difficulty about these historical views which
link the current situation to the remote past is that they create
a sense of fatalism and also confrontation which makes it difficult to achieve compromise and peaceful co-existence.[7]

How do we explain the continued use of history in Ireland?
Some of the reasons which were valid in the late nineteenth century are applicable today. Divisions over religion and nationalism
continue to be important and so many feel that historical expla-
nations remain valid. In our late twentieth century world, debates
over nationalism often include historical arguments. It is still true

that in the Anglo-American world in which we live, people find the historical approach the best way to understand our situation. The reality of the religious conflict in Ireland has often been ignored by historians and others in Ireland because it is not how things *ought* to be.[8] Perhaps this use of history has become a tradition in itself, part of the culture. For many people and political groupings in Ireland, north and south, history provides an ideology of sorts. Whatever the reasons for the prevalence of this historical approach it is clear that many are now aware of its dangers.

The Mitchell commission noted how because of these historical arguments about why the other side cannot be trusted 'even well-intentioned acts are often viewed with suspicion and hostility' and urged that 'what is really needed is the decommissioning of mind-sets in Northern Ireland.'[9] From various quarters this view has been echoed. Speaking in Dublin in November 1995 Deputy President F.W. De Klerk stated that an important element in the South African peace process was the acceptance that 'we would have to put the bitterness of the past behind us ...'[10] In a speech in June 1995, Mr Robert McCartney, M.P., criticised the use of history: 'when it becomes a catechism of past grievances, it is a corrosive curse which, in Ireland, has been refined into an art form.'[11] At a December 1995 launch of a book on Daniel O'Connell, Mr John Hume M.P. declared: 'If there is a lesson from Daniel O'Connell it is - the aislings [vision-poetry] of our ancestors should inspire us, not control us.'[12] Politicians still sometimes resort to the use of historical reference but clearly there is now a conscious effort to escape from the burden of the past, as contained in various myths.

Chapter five which dealt with commemorations, anniversaries and public holidays looked at how important events or individuals from the past have been remembered. It emphasised how in Ireland, as elsewhere, this concern for the past has been influenced by current interests. Chapter six on Irish identity showed how this concept has changed over time. The concluding chapter surveyed the writing of history in and on Northern Ireland. This new work is important. It allows us to understand the complexity of the past in its different dimensions. This historical approach is very different from the popular prescriptive view of the past, based on myths and heavily influenced by the present, which gives the past excessive influence on the contemporary world.

History is no more and no less important in Ireland than elsewhere. The current situation is not linked in a distinctive way to the past. The conflict in Northern Ireland is not an 'age-old one.' At the same time it is evident that historical myths are an important influence. These essays have drawn attention to how such myths have been created and how they are used. Ireland does not have a special history or unique problems, affected by its past. Other parts of Europe have also faced and still do face similar problems. As elsewhere, leaders and people in Ireland, both north and south, have a vital role to play in determining the shape of their own society, and are not just helpless victims of a turbulent past. The myths of history must not be allowed to unduly affect peoples' minds and influence their judgement. It is important that when people try to deal with the very real problems confronting them, they do so without the unnecessary and harmful burden of 'history's tune'.

Introduction

1 *Downing Street Declaration, December 1993,* (Linen Hall Library); *Belfast Telegraph,* 19 September 1995; *Belfast Telegraph,* 28 October 1993, *Belfast Newsletter,* 10 February 1995; *Irish Times,* 26 May 1995.
2 For a valuable discussion of Irish historical myths see R.J. Comerford 'Political myths in modern Ireland' in Princess Grace Irish Library, *Irishness in a changing society* (Gerrards Cross, 1988), pp 1–17; T.W. Moody 'Irish history and Irish mythology' in Ciaran Brady (ed.) *Interpreting Irish history* (Dublin, 1994), pp 71–86.
3 J. Bowyer Bell, *The Irish troubles: a generation of violence, 1967–92* (Dublin, 1993), p. 829.

Chapter 1: The unionist sense of history

1 *London Review of Books,* 5 April 1990.
2 Bill Rolston, *Politics and painting: murals and conflict in Northern Ireland* (Cranbury, New Jersey, 1991), p. 15.
3 *Belfast Newsletter,* 9–13 July 1790, 5–9 November 1790.
4 Anthony Buckley 'Uses of history among Ulster protestants' in Gerald Dawe and J.W. Foster (eds), *The poet's place: Ulster literature and society* (Belfast, 1991), p. 262.
5 Brian Lacy, *Siege city: the story of Derry and Londonderry* (Belfast, 1990), pp 154–8.
6 See B.M. Walker, *Sentry Hill: an Ulster farm and family* (Belfast, 1981; new edition, 1991), p. 63.
7 J.A. Froude, *The English in Ireland,* 3 volumes (London, 1872–4); Lord Macauley, *History of England* (London, 1864).
8 T.C. Barnard, 'The uses of 23 October and Irish protestant celebrations' in *English Historical Review,* cvi (1991), pp 889–920; and Jacqueline Hill, 'National festivals, the state and protestant ascendancy in Ireland, 1790–1829' in *Irish Historical Studies,* xxiv, no.93 (May, 1984), pp 30–5.
9 Hill, ibid: James Kelly, '"The glorious and immortal memory:" commemoration and protestant identity in Ireland, 1660–1800' in *Proceedings of the Royal Irish Academy,* section c (1994), pp 25–52.
10 Brian Lacy, *Siege city: the story of Derry and Londonderry* (Belfast, 1990), p. 171.
11 S.E. Long, *Orangeism in N. Ireland* (Belfast, n.d. approximately 1970).
12 R.J. McNeill, *Ulster's stand for union* (London, 1922), p. 13.
13 J.C. Beckett, *The making of modern Ireland* (London, 1966), p. 399; R.D. Jones, J.S. Kane, Robert Wallace, Douglas Sloan and Brian Courtney, *The Orange Citadel: a history of Orangeism in Portadown district* (Portadown, 1996), pp 26–30.

Hugh Shearman has described the importance, in this period of the first and second home rule bills, of 'the Orange organisation which had lingered in existence since the preceding century and which was now revived and expanded' *Ulster* (London, 1949) p. 130.

[14] Peter Francis, 'Franz Tieze (1842–1932) and the re-invention of history on glass' in the *Burlington Magazine* (May, 1994), pp 291–302.

[15] Eric Hobsbawm, 'Mass producing traditions: Europe, 1870–1914' in Eric Hobsbawm and Terence Ranger, *The invention of tradition* (Cambridge, 1983), pp 263–307.

[16] Thomas Witherow, *Derry and Enniskillen in the year 1689: the story of some famous battlefields in Ulster* (Belfast, 1873), p. viii.

[17] Thomas Macknight, *Ulster as it is, or, twenty eight years' experience as an Irish editor*, vol. I (London, 1896), pp 1–10. It is interesting to compare the highly critical views of Orange parades and the 12th of July commemorations in early editorials of the *Northern Whig* compared with later support for the event: *Northern Whig*, 14 July 1874 and 13 July 1893.

[18] Lord Ernest Hamilton, *The soul of Ulster* (London, 1917), pp 109–11.

[19] Richard McMinn, 'Presbyterianism and politics in Ulster, 1871–1900' in *Studia Hibernica, xx* (1981), pp 127–46.

[20] Quoted by McMinn, ibid, p. 131.

[21] In the case of St Patrick's church in Belfast, opened in 1815, see *Belfast Newsletter*, 7 March 1815, and in the case of Ballynahinch catholic church in 1868 see *Down Recorder*, 4 July 1868.

[22] J.A. Rentoul, *Stray thoughts and memories* (Dublin, 1921), pp 32–5.

[23] See Paul Bew and Frank Wright 'The agrarian opposition in Ulster politics, 1848–87' and B.M. Walker, 'The land question and elections in Ulster, 1868–86' in Samuel Clark and J.S. Donnelly (eds) *Irish peasants: violence and political unrest, 1780–1914* (Manchester, 1983), pp 192–270.

[24] See Donal Kerr, 'Religion, state and ethnic identity' in Donal Kerr (ed.) *Religion, state and ethnic groups* (Washington, 1992), pp 1–26. See especially pp 8–9 where Kerr quotes Norman Stone on this subject. See Gordon Smith, *Politics in Western Europe* (London, 1972; 4th edition, London, 1983), pp 18–26; Jan Erik Lane and S.O. Erson, *Politics and society in Western Europe* (London, 1987), pp 56–64, 97–9; J.H. Whyte, *Catholics in Western democracies* (Dublin, 1981), pp 47–75.

[25] See Alf Kaartvedt, 'The economic basis of Norwegian nationalism in the nineteenth century' in Rosalind Mitchison (ed.) *The roots of nationalism: studies in Northern Europe* (Edinburgh, 1980), pp 11–19; Gordon Smith, *Politics in Western Europe* (London, 1972; 4th edition, 1983), pp 297–302, 308–10.

[26] A. Lijphart, *The politics of accommodation: pluralism and democracy in the Netherlands* (Berkeley, second edition, 1975).

[27] Estyn Evans, *Northern Ireland* (London, 1951), as quoted in M.W. Dewar, John Brown and S.E. Long, *Orangeism: a new historical appreciation* (Belfast, 1967), p. 17.

[28] T.W. Moody, 'Irish history and Irish mythology' in Ciaran Brady, *Interpreting Irish history* (Dublin, 1994), pp 84–5.

Chapter 2: A milestone in Irish history

[1] For a more detailed study of these elections see B.M. Walker, *Ulster politics: the formative years 1868–86* (Belfast, 1989); C.C. O'Brien, *Parnell and his party, 1880–90* (Oxford, 1957); and James Loughlin, *Gladstone, home rule and the Ulster question, 1882–93* (Dublin, 1986).

[2] All information on election results has come from B.M. Walker, *Parliamentary election results in Ireland, 1801–1922* (Dublin, 1978).

[3] Mary Daly, *Industrial development and Irish national identity, 1922–39*, (Dublin, 1992), p. 3.

[4] B.M. Walker, 'The Irish electorate, 1868–1915' in *I.H.S.*, xvii, no. 71 (Mar. 1973), pp 359–406.

[5] *Belfast Morning News*, 10 November 1885.

[6] See W.E. Vaughan and A. J. Fitzpatrick (eds), *Irish historical statistics: population, 1821–1971* (Dublin, 1978)

[7] See B.M. Walker, Mary O'Dowd and Ciaran Brady (eds), *Ulster: an illustrated history* (London, 1989), p. 164.

[8] W.E. Vaughan, *Landlords and tenants in Ireland, 1848–1904* (Dublin, 1984).

[9] Vaughan and Fitzpatrick (eds) *Irish historical statistics: population 1821–1971*, pp 57–9.

[10] See Walker, *Ulster politics*, pp 15–38; David Hempton and Myrtle Hill, *Evangelical protestantism in Ulster society, 1740–1890* (London, 1992); Emmet Larkin, 'The devotional revolution in Ireland, 1850–75' in *American Historical Review*, lxxvii, no. 3 (June 1972), pp 625–52.

[11] *Weekly Examiner*, 13 March 1886.

[12] Walker, *Ulster politics*, p. 26. A.C. Hepburn 'Work, class and religion in Belfast, 1871–1911' in *Irish Economic and Social History*, x (1983), p. 50.

[13] Walker, 'The Irish electorate, 1868–1915' pp 359–406.

[14] Walker, *Ulster politics*, p. 154.

[15] O'Brien, *Parnell*, p. 150.

[16] Ibid., p. 133.

[17] Emmet Larkin, 'Church, state and nation in modern Ireland' in *American Historical Review*, lxxx, no. 4 (Oct. 1975), pp 1265–7.

[18] Walker, *Ulster politics*, p. 204; Michael Davitt, *The fall of feudalism in Ireland* (London, 1904), pp 466–9.

[19] A.C. Murray, 'Nationality and local politics in late nineteenth-century Ireland: the case of County Westmeath' in *I.H.S.*, xxv, no. 98 (November 1986) p. 146.

[20] Walker, *Ulster politics*, p. 213.

[21] P. J. Buckland, *Irish unionism, 1885–1923* (Belfast, 1973), pp 95–9.

[22] B.M. Walker, 'Party organisation in Ulster, 1865–92: registration agents and their activities' in Peter Roebuck (ed.) *Plantation to partition: essays in Ulster history in honour of J.L. McCracken* (Belfast, 1981), pp 201–3.

[23] E.G., D.C. Savage, 'The origins of the Ulster unionist party, 1885–6' in *I.H.S*, xii, no. 47 (March 1961), p. 186.

[24] Walker, *Ulster politics*, pp 177–92.

[25] Ibid., p. 179.

[26] Ibid., p. 203.

[27] Ibid., pp 207–8.

[28] Ibid., p. 202.

[29] T.M. Healy, *Letters and leaders of my day* (2 vols, London, 1928), i, pp 231–3.

[30] Walker, *Ulster politics*, pp 190, 209–11.

[31] Ibid., pp 215–9.

[32] P.J.O. McCann, 'The protestant home rule movement, 1886–95' (MA thesis, UCD, 1972); see also James Loughlin, 'The Irish protestant home rule association' in *I.H.S*, xxiv, no. 95 (May 1985), pp 341–60.

[33] James Anderson, 'Ideological variations in Ulster during Ireland's first home rule crisis: an analysis of local newspapers' in C.H. Williams and E. Kofman (eds) *Community conflict, partition and nationalism* (London, 1989), pp 133–66.

[34] For valuable discussions of these movements see D.G. Boyce, *Nationalism in Ireland* (London, 1982; new edition, 1991) and Alvin Jackson, *The Ulster party: Irish unionists in the House of Commons, 1884–1911)* (Oxford, 1989).

[35] Emmet Larkin, 'Church, state and nation in modern Ireland' in *American Historical Review*, lxxx, no. 4 (Oct. 1975), p. 1267.

[36] See A.T.Q. Stewart, *The narrow ground: aspects of Ulster1609–1969* (London, 1977; new edition 1989), p. 163; John Coakley 'The foundations of statehood' in John Coakely and Michael Gallagher (eds), *Politics in the republic of Ireland*, (Galway 1992), p. 8; Tom Garvin 'Democratic politics in independent Ireland' in ibid., p. 222.

[37] See S.M. Lipset and Stein Rokkan, 'Cleavage structures, party systems and vote alignment: an introduction' in Lipset and Rokkan (eds), *Party systems and voter alignment* (New York, 1967), pp 50–6; Gordon Smith, *Politics in Western Europe* (London, 1972; 4th edition, London, 1983), pp 12–14, 44–6; A.R. Ball, *Modern politics and government* (London, 1988), pp 82–4.

[38] See Smith, *Politics in Western Europe* pp 18–26; Jan Erik Lane and S.O. Erson, *Politics and society in Western Europe* (London, 1987), pp 56–64, 97–9; J.H. Whyte, *Catholics in Western democracies* (Dublin, 1981), pp 47–75.

[39] See Alf Kaartvedt, 'The economic basis of Norwegian nationalism in the nineteenth century' in Rosalind Mitchison (ed.), *The roots of nationalism: studies in Northern Europe* (Edinburgh, 1980), pp 11–19; Gordon Smith, *Politics in Western Europe*, pp 297–302, 308–10.

Chapter 3: Irish problems and European comparisons

[1] Sir Kenneth Bloomfield, *Stormont in crisis: a memoir* (Belfast, 1994), p. 66.

[2] James O'Connell, 'Northern Ireland: the role of religion in a political conflict', in *Furrow*, xlii, no. 1 (January 1991), p. 55.

[3] Jurg Steiner, *European democracies* (New York, 1995 third edition), p. 309.

[4] J.H. Whyte, *Understanding Northern Ireland*, pp 175–93.

[5] *Irish News*, 6 September 1921, reported in *Irish News*, 6 September 1988.

[6] Lord Ernest Hamilton, *The soul of Ulster* (London, 1917), p. 192.

[7] *Parliamentary debates, Northern Ireland* (Commons) xvi (1933–4), pp 613–28.

[8] A.T.Q. Stewart, *The narrow ground: aspects of Ulster 1609–1969* (London, 1977), p. 180.

[9] *Annual report of the Community Relations Council*, 1993, p. 15.

[10] *Irish Times*, 4 April 1995.

[11] Steve Bruce, *The edge of the union: the Ulster Loyalist political vision* (Oxford, 1994), p. 22.

[12] *Irish Times*, 2 December 1991.

[13] Ibid., 13 April 1995.

[14] Richard Rose and Derek Unwin, 'Social cohesion, parties and strains in regimes' in *Comparative political studies* 11 (April, 1969), pp 7–67. See also Richard Rose (ed.) *Electoral behaviour – a comparative handbook* (London, 1974), especially chapters by Rose.

164   NOTES FOR PAGES 38–50

[15] Gordon Smith, *Politics in Western Europe: a comparative analysis* (London, 1972; 5th edition, 1989), pp 19–28.

[16] Ibid., p. 22.

[17] Ibid., pp 24–6.

[18] Ibid, p. 26–8.

[19] Quoted in ibid., p. 27.

[20] Yves Mény, *Government and politics in Western Europe* (Paris, 1987: Oxford, 1990, translation), pp 21–2.

[21] Ibid., pp 28–9.

[22] Smith, *Western European politics* pp 12–15, 41–4.

[23] Arend Lijphart, *Democracy in plural societies: a comparative exploration* (Yale, 1977), pp 21–99) and *The politics of accommodation: pluralism and democracy in the Netherlands* (Berkeley, second edition, 1975).

[24] Mény, *Government and politics in Western Europe* p. 17.

[25] Ronald McNeill, *Ulster's stand for union* (London, 1922), p. 9.

[26] Smith, *Politics in Western Europe* p. 22.

[27] John Bowman, 'The wolf in sheep's clothing: Richard Hayes's proposal for a new national library of Ireland, 1959–60' in R.J. Hill and Michael Marsh (eds)', *Modern Irish democracy: essays in honour of Basil Chubb* (Dublin, 1993), pp 44–61.

[28] Quoted by D.A. Kerr 'Religion, state and ethnic identity', in idem (ed.), *Religion, state and ethnic groups* (London, 1992), pp 8–9.

[29] Archbishop Walsh to Tobias Kirby, 26 September 1885 in P.J. Corish (ed.) 'Kirby Papers, Irish College Rome' in *Archivum Hibernicum,* xxxii, 1974, p. 4.

[30] See Tom Garvin, *Nationalist revolutionaries in Ireland 1858–1928* (Oxford, 1987), especially pp 57–77 and 125–30; see also C.C. O'Brien, *Ancestral voices* (Dublin 1994).

[31] Patrick Maume, *History Ireland,* ii, no. 3 (Autumn, 1994). p. 30.

[32] Eamon Phoenix, *Northern nationalism: nationalist politics, partition and the catholic minority in Northern Ireland, 1890–1940* (Belfast, 1994), pp 49–51.

[33] See B.M. Walker, *Ulster politics: the formative years, 1868–86* (Belfast, 1989), pp 177–91.

[34] Paul Bew, *Ideology and the Irish question: Ulster unionism and Irish nationalism, 1912–16* (Oxford 1994), pp 68–9.

[35] J.A. Rentoul, *Stray thoughts and memories* (Dublin, 1921), pp 213–5.

[36] *Northern Whig,* 30 September 1912.

[37] Quotes from Dennis Kennedy, *The widening gulf: northern attitudes to the independent Irish state, 1919–49* (Belfast, 1988), p. 166, and *Debates of the parliament of Northern Ireland,* xvi, 1933–4, 1095.

[38] Mary Harris, *The catholic church and the foundation of the Northern Irish state* (Cork, 1993), p. 3.

[39] Church and government committee of the presbyterian church in Ireland, *Presbyterian principles and political witness in Northern Ireland* (Belfast, 1993), p. 7.

[40] Fionnuala O'Connor, *In search of a state: catholics in Northern Ireland* (Belfast, 1993), pp 172–4, 288–9, 301, 372–3.

[41] Harris, *Catholic church*, p. 3.

[42] Cited, ibid., p. 6.

[43] Quoted in Dermot Keogh, *Ireland and the Vatican: the politics and diplomacy of church-state relations, 1922–60* (Cork, 1994), pp 29–30.

[44] Ibid., p. 315.

[45] Ibid., pp 366–9.

[46] Survey in 1993 for the Irish Council of Churches, reported in the *Belfast Telegraph*, 28 March 1995.

[47] Church and government committee of the presbyterian church in Ireland, *Presbyterian principles and political witness in Northern Ireland* (Belfast, 1993), p. 6.

[48] Interview of Pádraig O'Malley by Barry White in *Belfast Telegraph*, 5 January 1995: Padraig O'Malley, 'The question of religion' in *Fortnight*, February 1995, pp 22–7.

[49] Lecture on religion and conflict by Cardinal Cahal Daly to the Armagh together – international conference on religion and conflict, reported in the *Armagh Observer*, 26 May 1994.

[50] *Observer*, April 12, 1992.

[51] C.C. O'Brien, *Irish Independent*, 5 March, 1995.

Chapter 4: The use and abuse of history in Ireland today

[1] Speech of Rev. Ian Paisley, 25 November 1995 (typescript, Linen Hall Library).

[2] *An Phoblacht* 25 June 1992.

[3] *Irish Times*, 17 February 1996.

[4] Edna O'Brien, *House of splendid isolation* (London, 1994), p. 3.

[5] Leon Uris, *Trinity* (London, 1976), p. 751.

[6] Dermot Bolger, 'Shift your shadow or I'll bust you' in *Sunday Independent*, 16 August 1992.

[7] A.T.Q. Stewart, *The narrow ground: aspects of Ulster, 1609–1969* (London, 1977), p. 16.

[8] See Patrick O'Farrell, *England and Ireland since 1800* (Oxford, 1975) Oliver Macdonagh, *States of mind: two centuries of Anglo-Irish conflict, 1780–1980* (London, 1983; 1992 edition), pp 1–14: Roy Foster, *Paddy and Mr Punch: connections in Irish and English history* (London, 1993), pp 1–20.

9 *Irish Times*, 30 August, 1993.

10 Jack Magee, 'Response to paper by Roy Foster on varieties of Irishness' in Maurna Crozier (ed.) *Cultural traditions in Northern Ireland.*

11 "See his contribution in the Churches Central Committee for Community Work, *Irish history, fact or fiction* (Belfast, 1976).

12 *Irish Times*, 25 February, 1995.

13 Eric Hobsbawm and Terence Ranger, *The invention of tradition* (Cambridge, 1983): Ciaran Brady, *Ideology and the historians. Historical Studies xvii* (Dublin, 1992).

14 Mason Wade, *The French Canadians 1760–1967* (Toronto, 1968), i, p. 1.

15 See Leonard Thomson, *The political mythology of apartheid* (New Haven, 1985). I am grateful to Adrian Guelke for this point.

16 See speech of F.W. De Clerk to Dublin forum, 21 November 1995 (typescript, Linen Hall Library).

17 Sean Lemass 'The next fifty years' in *The Irish Digest*, lxxxvi, no.4, June, 1966, p. 9.

18 This point was also made in a paper on Irish science by Professor Richard Kearney at the International Tyndall School, *Irish Times*, 15 September 1993.

19 J.J. Lee, *Ireland 1912–85* (Cambridge, 1989), pp 513–14.

20 Dermot Bolger, 'Shift your shadow or I'll burst you' in *Sunday Independent*, 16 August, 1992.

21 John Whyte, *Interpreting Northern Ireland* (Oxford, 1990), pp 177–9; Brian Walker, 'Ireland's historical position – 'Colonial' or 'European' in *Irish Review*, no.9 (Autumn), 1990, pp 36–40.

22 Frank McDonald, *The destruction of Dublin* (Dublin, 1985), p. 12.

23 *Irish Times*, 20 February 1996.

24 From editorial in the *Irish Arts Review*, xi, (1995) p. 51.

25 Quoted in *Irish Times*, 27 April 1992.

26 *Irish Independent*, 4 April 1993.

27 *Irish Times*, 18 August 1992.

28 Ibid., 11 October 1994.

29 *Sunday Times*, 17 October 1993.

30 Margaret Thatcher, *The Downing Street years* (London, 1993), p. 400.

31 *Observer*, 18 September 1994.

32 *Irish Independent*, 14 November 1992.

33 *Irish Times*, 17 March 1993.

34 *Ibid.*, 5 April 1993.

35 *Irish Independent*, 19 April 1993.

36 *Irish Independent*, 19 June and 8 October 1993.

37 *Irish Times*, 8 November 1993.

[38] *Downing Street Declaration* (Linen Hall Library).

[39] *Sunday Independent,* 19 December 1993.

[40] *The Irish troubles* p. 829.

[41] Richard Davis, *Mirror hate: the convergent ideology of Northern Ireland paramilitaries, 1966–92* (Aldershot, 1994), p. 3.

[42] Shane O'Doherty, *The volunteer: a former I.R.A. man's true story* (London, 1993), pp 27–30.

[43] Pádraig O'Malley, *Biting at the grave: the Irish hunger strikes and the politics of despair* (Boston, 1990).

[44] *Irish Independent,* 25–8 December 1992; *Irish Times,* 23 March 1993.

[45] *Belfast Telegraph,* 2 July 1992.

[46] *Irish Times,* 18 December 1993.

[47] *Irish Independent,* 19 April 1993.

[48] *Church of Ireland Gazette,* 13 January 1995.

[49] See *New Ulster Defender,* October 1993.

[50] *Hansard,* lxxxvii, (1985–6) 779, 783, 904 and 907.

[51] *Belfast Telegraph,* 28 October 1993: *Belfast Newsletter,* 10 February 1995.

[52] Steve Bruce, T*he red hand* (Oxford, 1992).

[53] Alvin Jackson, 'Unionist myths 1912–85' in *Past and Present* no.136 (August, 1992), pp 164–85.

[54] *Irish News,* 28 December 1992.

[55] Ibid., 18 July 1992.

[56] Ibid., 2 October 1993.

[57] *Observer,* 4 September 1994.

[58] *Irish Times,* 13 April 1994.

[59] *Sunday Times,* 5 March 1995.

[60] *Combat,* October 1994.

[61] *Irish News,* 1 September 1994.

[62] *An Phoblacht,* 13 April 1995, 28 March 1991.

[63] *Belfast Newsletter,* 26 May 1995.

Chapter 5: Commemorations, festivals and public holidays

[1] Diaspora speech, 2 February 1995, issued by government information office.

[2] Reported in *The Times,* 26 December 1995.

[3] Edna Longley, *The living stream: literature and revisionism in Ireland* Newcastle-upon-Tyne, 1994), p. 69.

[4] These contrasts are pointed out by Jacqueline Hill, 'National festivals, the state and "protestant ascendancy"' in *Irish Historical Studies,* xxiv, no. 93 (May, 1984), p. 30.

[5] *Irish Times,* 18 March 1994.

[6] Information on first St Patrick's Day from John Crimmins, quoted by Pauline Mooney, 'A symbol for the nation: the national holiday campaign, 1901–3 (MA thesis, 1992, St Patrick's College, Maynooth) p. 20 (hereafter cited as Mooney, *The national holiday*); information on denominational make up of Americans of Irish ancestry from D.H. Akenson, *The Irish diaspora: a primer* (Belfast, 1994), pp 219–24.

[7] Charles Doherty, 'The problem of St Patrick' in *History Ireland*, iii, no.1 (Spring 1995), p. 15.

[8] *Irish Independent*, 18 March 1981 and *Irish News*, 18 March 1988.

[9] Hill, *National festivals*, pp 30–51.

[10] For an account of the Order of St Patrick see Peter Galloway, *The most illustrious Order of St Patrick* (London, 1983).

[11] Hill, *National festivals*, p. 48.

[12] See *Northern Whig*, 19 March 1878 and 18 March 1884.

[13] Quoted in Peter Alter, 'Symbols of Irish nationalism' in Alan O'Day (ed.), *Reactions to Irish nationalism* (Dublin, 1987), p. 10.

[14] *Northern Whig*, 18 March 1890.

[15] *Freeman's Journal*, 18 March 1890.

[16] St Patrick's Day in the USA is discussed later in this chapter. For Australia see Oliver MacDonagh, 'Irish culture and nationalism translated: St Patrick's Day, 1888, in Australia' in Oliver MacDonagh, W.F. Mandle and Pauric Travers (eds) *Irish culture and nationalism, 1750–1950* (Canberra, 1984), pp 69–82.

[17] Mooney, *The national holiday*.

[18] Quote in ibid., p. 76.

[19] *Irish News*, 17 March 1910.

[20] *Irish Independent*, 18 March 1926.

[21] Ibid, 19 March 1934.

[22] Ibid, 18 March 1935.

[23] *Northern Whig*, 18 March 1939.

[24] See for example, *Belfast Newsletter*, 18 March 1926 and *Northern Whig*, 18 March 1935.

[25] *Irish News*, 18 March 1932 and *Belfast Newsletter*, 17 March 1932.

[26] Rex Cathcart, *The most contrary region: the B.B.C. in Northern Ireland, 1924–84* (Belfast, 1984), p. 32.

[27] Lyn Gallagher, *The Grand Opera House, Belfast* (Belfast, 1995), p. 55.

[28] *Irish Times*, 20 January 1996.

[29] See *Irish Independent*, 18 March 1948, 17 March 1949, 18 March 1950, 17 and 18 March 1953 and 19 March 1956.

[30] See ibid., and *Irish Independent* 19 March 1962.

[31] *Capuchin Annual*, (1962) p. 218.

[32] See *Belfast Newsletter*, 16 March 1961.

[33] See ibid., 17 March 1961.

[34] Document is quoted in *Belfast Newsletter*, 1 January 1996.

[35] *Belfast Telegraph*, 17 March 1956.

[36] Maurice Hayes, *Minority verdict: experiences of a catholic public servant* (Belfast, 1995), pp 29–30.

[37] *Irish Independent*, 18 March 1971, 18 March 1983, 18 March 1987.

[38] Ibid., 17 March 1972.

[39] *Irish Times*, 19 January 1996.

[40] *Irish Independent*, 18 March 1974 and 18 March 1977.

[41] Ibid., 18 March 1985, *Belfast Telegraph*, 18 March 1990.

[42] *Irish Independent*, 18 March 1985, *Belfast Telegraph*, 17 March 1990.

[43] Alannah Hopkin, *The living legend of St Patrick* (London, 1989), p. 123.

[44] Cited in Mooney, *The national holiday*, pp 22–6.

[45] Kenneth Moss, 'St Patrick's Day celebrations and the formation of Irish-American identity, 1845–75' in *Journal of Social History* (Fall, 1995) xxix, no. 1, pp 125–48.

[46] For Boston see T.H. O'Connor, *The Boston Irish: a political history* (Boston, 1995).

[47] See comments by Conor Cruise O'Brien, *Irish Independent*, 18 March 1995.

[48] Hopkin, S*t Patrick* p. 131.

[49] *Irish Times*, 18 March 1994.

[50] *Irish Independent*, 18 March 1995; *Irish Times*, 18 March 1995.

[51] Information on this event in the next section comes from Rosemary Ryan (et al) 'Commemorating 1916' in *Retrospect* (1984), pp 59–62 (hereafter cited as *Retrospect: 1916*). This article looked at how the event had been commemorated at each decade since 1916. My main newspaper source for this event in the south has been the *Irish Independent*.

[52] Sean McCann (ed.) *The world of Brendan Behan* (London, 1965), p. 32.

[53] *Irish News*, 1 April 1929.

[54] Ibid, 21 April 1930, 6 April 1931, 28 March 1932, 17 April 1933.

[55] Ibid, 6 April 1942.

[56] *Irish Independent*, 14 April 1942.

[57] Ibid.

[58] *Retrospect: 1916*, p. 61.

[59] *Irish Independent*, 19 April 1954.

[60] *Retrospect: 1916*, p. 61.

[61] Ibid., p. 61.

[62] *Irish Independent*, 3 April 1972.

[63] For comment on these see Máirín Ní Dhonnchadha and Theo Dorgan (eds) *Revising the rising* (Derry, 1991).

64 *Irish News*, 10 April 1950.

65 Ibid, 10 April 1950, 26 March 1951, 2 April 1956.

66 *Belfast Telegraph*, 12 and 18 April 1966.

67 *Irish Independent*, 3 April 1972.

68 *An Phoblacht*, 25 April 1981.

69 Ibid., 13 April 1995.

70 Hill, *National festivals*, pp 33–4. For further information on commemoration of William in the eighteenth century see James Kelly, "The glorious and immortal memory": commemoration and protestant identity in Ireland, 1660–1800' in *Proceedings of the Royal Irish Academy*, section C (1994), pp 25–52.

71 *Belfast Newsletter*, 9–13 July 1790.

72 Hereward Senior, *Orangeism in Ireland and Britain, 1795–1836* (London, 1966), pp 38–41.

73 Ibid., pp 1–21; M.W. Dewar, John Brown and S.E. Long (eds), *Orangeism, a new historical appreciation* (Belfast, 1967), pp 71–107; Jim Smyth, 'The men of no popery: the origins of the Orange Order' in *History Ireland*, iii, no. 3 (Autumn, 1995), pp 48–53; Andrew Boyd, 'The Orange Order, 1795–1995' in *History Today*, xlv, no. 9 (September 1995), pp 16–23.

74 Jack Johnston, *From Annahoe to Fivemiletown: Orangeism in the Clogher Valley* (Clogher, 1995), p. 6

75 *Belfast Newsletter*, 19 July 1822.

76 Aiken McClelland, 'The Orange Order in Co Monaghan' in *Clogher Record* (1978) p. 387.

77 Senior, *Orangeism*, pp 177–215; Hill, *National festivals*, pp 41–8.

78 McClelland, *Orange Order*, p. 392.

79 R.D. Jones, J.S. Kane, Robert Wallace, Douglas Sloan, Brian Courtney, T*he Orange citadel: a history of Orangeism in Portadown district* (Portadown, 1996), pp 19–20.

80 Jonathan Bardon, *A history of Ulster* (Belfast, 1992), pp 302–4.

81 *The Orange citadel*, p. 20.

82 See Aiken McClelland, *William Johnston of Ballykilbeg* (Lurgan, 1990).

83 *The Orange citadel*, pp 23–4.

84 This figure is from C.J. Houston and W.J. Smyth, 'Transferred loyalties: Orangeism in the United States and Ontario' in *American Review of Canadian Studies*, (Summer 1984), p. 894, as cited by S.E. Long in *Steadfast for faith and freedom: 200 years of Orangeism* (Belfast, 1990), p. 67.

85 *A brief history of Omagh District L.O.L no.11, 1795–1995* (hereafter cited as *Omagh District L.O.L*) (Omagh, 1995), p. 21.

86 *A celebration 1690–1990: the Orange institution* (Belfast, 1990), pp 29 and 65.

[87] Information from Belinda Loftus, author of *Mirrors, William III and Mother Ireland* (Dundrum, 1990): Orange street arches seem to have been erected from the early nineteenth century, but Orange wall murals only appeared in the early 1900s (see Alvin Jackson, 'Irish unionist imagery, 1850–1920' in Eve Patton (ed) *Returning to ourselves: second volume of Hewitt summer school papers* (Belfast, 1995), p. 350).

[88] *Omagh District L.O.L.*, p. 63.

[89] Ibid., p. 12.

[90] Johnston, *Clogher Valley Orangeism*, p. 22.

[91] *Orangeism: a new historical appreciation*, pp 138–40; *Londonderry Journal*, 8 August 1868.

[92] Examination of early 1870s demonstrations compared with those in 1848 suggests this; *Belfast Newsletter*, 13 July 1849 and 14 July 1872.

[93] J.C. Beckett, *The making of modern Ireland* (London, 1966), p. 399.

[94] See Aiken McClelland, 'The later Orange Order' in T.W. Williams (ed) *Secret societies in Ireland* (Dublin, 1973), pp 128–31.

[95] At earlier parades in the late 1840s this does not seem to have happened. *Belfast Newsletter*, 14 July 1872.

[96] See *Orangeism: a historical appreciation*, p. 154, and McClelland, *Later Orange Order*, p. 133.

[97] Quoted in *The Orange citadel*, p. 34.

[98] *Northern Ireland Parliament*, vol II, 15 July 1922.

[99] Ibid, vol VI, 19 May 1925.

[100] Speeches quoted in Bardon, *Ulster*, p. 538.

[101] Quoted in *The Orange citadel*, p. 36.

[102] Bardon, *Ulster*, pp 539–40.

[103] McClelland, *Orange Order*, p. 402.

[104] *Belfast Newsletter*, 13 July 1949 and 13 July 1955.

[105] Quoted in *The Orange citadel*, p. 42.

[106] Bardon, *Ulster*, p. 609.

[107] *A celebration, 1690–1990: the Orange Institution* (Belfast, 1990), pp 12–13 and 82.

[108] For valuable analysis of the significance of the 12th July parades see Dominic Bryan, 'Interpreting the twelfth' in *History Ireland*, ii, no.2 (summer, 1994), pp 37–41; introduction by W.J. Smyth to catalogue, *Echoes: paintings by George Fleming: The twelfth of July*, produced for exhibition in St Patrick's College, Maynooth, 1995.

[109] Keith Jeffery, 'The Great War in modern Irish memory' in T.G. Fraser and Keith Jeffery (eds.), *Men, women and war: historical studies xviii* (Dublin, 1993), pp 136–57, and Jane Leonard, 'Facing the 'fin-

ger of scorn': veterans' memories of Ireland after the Great War' in M. Evans and K. Lunn (eds) *War and memory in the twentieth century* (Oxford, 1996), pp 1–11.

110 See, for example, *Irish Times*, 12 November 1925.

111 *Belfast Telegraph*, 11 November 1924.

112 Jeffery, *The Great War*, p. 85.

113 *Irish News*, 12 November, 1924.

114 *Irish Times*, 12 November, 1925.

115 *Belfast Newsletter*, 12 November 1937. This was partly a result of general government concern about parades in Ireland, including the I.R.A. and Blueshirt marches.

116 Jane Leonard, 'Lest we forget, Irish war memorials' in David Fitzpatrick (ed.) *Ireland and the First World War* (Dublin, 1986), p. 64.

117 Leonard, *Veterans' memories*, p. 11.

118 Jeffery, *The Great War*, p. 150–1.

119 *Irish News*, 12 November 1924; Jeffery, *The Great War* pp 151 and 156

120 Jeffery, *The Great War*, pp 150–1.

121 *Belfast Telegraph*, 12 November 1930; *Belfast Newsletter*, 11 November 1937. Nationalist participation in Armistice Day ceremonies is currently being researched by Jane Leonard as part of a larger project on twentieth century conflict commemoration in Northern Ireland.

122 *Irish News*, 5 May 1995.

123 *Belfast Newsletter*, 12 and 13 November 1950, and 7 November 1955 and 11 November 1958.

124 *Belfast Newsletter*, 13 November 1950.

125 Leonard, *Veterans' memories*, pp 8–9.

126 For account of 1982 controversy see comments by former president Patrick Hillery, *Irish Times*, 3 August 1991.

127 Leonard, *Veterans' memories*, p. 9.

128 Ibid. See comments by Kevin Myers on Islandbridge opening, *Irish Times* 2 July 1994.

129 Marianne Elliott, *Wolfe Tone: prophet of Irish independence* (New Haven, 1989), pp 411–19.

130 Ibid., p. 417.

131 See *Irish Independent*, 25 June 1923, 24 June 1924; *Irish Times*, 20 June 1932, 10 June 1933, 25 June 1934, 20 June 1966.

132 Aiken McClelland, *William Johnston of Ballykilbeg* (Lurgan, 1990), pp 70–3.

133 Ibid.

134 *Sunday Tribune*, 13 August 1995.

135 See M.T.Foy, The ancient order of Hibernians: an Irish political religious pressure group, 1884–1975 (MA thesis, 1976 Queen's Univerisity of Belfast).

136 Eamon Phoenix, *Northern nationalism* (Belfast, 1994) p. 5.

137 Foy, *Hibernians,* p. 160.

138 *Irish Times,* 29 January 1996.

139 W.C. Lyttle, *Betsy Gray, or, Hearts of Down* (Bangor, 1896; reprint, Newcastle, 1968, with added material), pp 162–3.

140 Article by Yvonne Healy in *Irish Times,* 21 July 1995.

Chapter 6: Irish identity

1 Report of 1993 social attitude survey in *Irish Times,* 19 May 1995.

2 David Hayton, 'Anglo-Irish attitudes: changing perceptions of national identity among the protestant ascendancy in Ireland, ca.1690–1750' in *Studies in Eighteenth Century Culture,* xvii (1987), pp 145–57.

3 *Irish Times,* 31 January 1994.

4 Quoted in D.G. Boyce, *Nationalism in Ireland* (London, 1982; second edition, 1991), p. 149.

5 Quoted in J.C. Beckett, *The Anglo-Irish tradition* (London, 1976), p. 10.

6 Quoted in A.T.Q. Stewart, *A deeper silence: the hidden origins of the United Kingdom* (London, 1993), p. 130.

7 Boyce, *Nationalism,* p. 127.

8 Thomas Davis, *Literary and historical essays* (New York, 1868), p. 222: *Poems of Thomas Davis* (New York 1868), p. 53.

9 For the reference to Cullen see Boyce, *Nationalism,* p. 180: for the reference to Biggar see F. Healey, 'J G Biggar' in *Clio,* (1969), p. 12.

10 Quoted in John A. Murphy 'Religion and Irish identity' in Princess Grace Irish Library (ed), *Irishness in a changing society* (Gerrards Cross, 1988), p. 133.

11 Quoted in L.G. Redmond-Howard, *John Redmond: the man and the demand* (London, 1912), p. 226.

12 Quoted in D.G. Boyce 'Trembling solicitude: Irish conservatism, nationality and public opinion, 1833–86' in D.G. Boyce, Robert Eccleshall and Vincent Geoghegan (eds) *Political thought in Ireland since the seventeenth century* (London, 1993), p. 133.

13 *Northern Whig,* 5 November 1868.

14 Thomas Hamilton, *History of the Irish presbyterian church* (Edinburgh, 1886, second edition, 1887), pp 1–2. By 1900 it was claimed that this book had sold 30,000 copies (James Dewar (ed), *History of the Elmwood presbyterian church* (Belfast, 1900), p. 145).

15 *Ulster Unionist Convention of 1892: report of proceedings* (Belfast, 1892).

16 *Unionist Convention for provinces of Leinster, Munster and Connaught, 1892* (Dublin, 1892), p. 61.

[17] See Tom Hennessey 'Ulster unionist territorial and national identities 1886–93: province, island, kingdom and empire' in *Irish Political Studies*, viii, 1993, pp 21–36.

[18] An exception, quoted a number of times in histories of the presbyterian church, was the statement by Moderator William Park to the presbyterian general assembly in 1890: 'seldom if ever, have any of us been ashamed to declare that we are Britons', Finlay Holmes, *Our Irish presbyterian heritage* (Belfast, 1985), p. 136. However, as Professor Finlay Holmes has informed me, this reference to 'Britons' is a misquote.

[19] *Northern Whig* 1 October 1912.

[20] *Hansard*, xxxvii, 219 (1912).

[21] Keith Haines, *Neither rogues nor fools: a history of Campbell College and Campbellians* (Belfast, 1993), p. 149.

[22] *Northern Whig* 24 October 1910; *Hansard*, xxxvii, 1091 (1912).

[23] Alvin Jackson, 'Irish unionism, 1905–21' in Peter Collins (ed.), *Nationalism and unionism: conflict in Ireland, 1885–1921* (Belfast, 1994), pp 44–5.

[24] Gearóid O'Tuathaigh, 'The Irish-Ireland idea: rationale and relevance' in Edna Longley (ed) *Culture in Ireland: division or diversity* (Belfast, 1991).

[25] Quoted in Paul Bew, *Conflict and conciliation in Ireland, 1890–1910* (Oxford, 1987), p. 13.

[26] Robert Lynd, *Home life in Ireland* (London, 1909), pp 1–2.

[27] Quoted in Tony Hepburn *Conflict of nationality in modern Ireland* (London, 1980), pp 64–5.

[28] Ibid., p. 65. See D.H. Harkness, 'Nation, state and national identity in Ireland' in Princess Grace Library (ed) *Irishness in a changing society*, pp 127–9.

[29] Quoted in Richard Rose, *Governing without consensus: an Irish perspective* (London, 1971) p. 203.

[30] Quoted in Ruth Dudley Edwards, *Patrick Pearse: the triumph of failure* (London, 1977), p. 260.

[31] John Bowman, *De Valera and the Ulster question, 1911–1973* (Oxford, 1982), p. 32.

[32] *Northern Whig* 23 June 1921.

[33] O'Tuathaigh, 'The Irish-Ireland idea'; Clare O'Halloran, *Partition and the limits of Irish nationalism* (Dublin, 1987); R.F. Foster, *Modern Ireland 1600–1972* (London, 1988), pp 518–9.

[34] Dennis Kennedy, *The widening gulf: northern attitudes to the independent Irish state 1919–49* p. 167.

[35] Ibid., p. 184.

36 W.E. Vaughan, *Irish historical statistics: population, 1821–1971* (Dublin, 1978), pp 68, 73 and 49.

37 Quoted by Roy Foster in *Times Literary Supplement*, 1 October 1993.

38 Quoted in J.C. Beckett, *The Anglo-Irish tradition* (London, 1976), pp 148–9.

39 See Kennedy, *The widening gulf* p. 61; and Patrick Buckland, *The factory of grievances: devolved government in Northern Ireland, 1921–39* (Dublin, 1979).

40 See D.H. Akenson, *A mirror to Kathleen's face: education in independent Ireland, 1922–60* (Kingston, 1975), Kennedy, *The widening gulf*, p. 182.

41 Lecture by John Birt, reported in the *Irish Independent*, 4 February 1995.

42 See Mary Harris, *The catholic church and the foundation of the Northern Irish state* (Cork, 1993); Eamon Phoenix, *Northern nationalism: nationalist politics, partition and the catholic minority in Northern Ireland, 1890–1940* (Belfast, 1994).

43 Quoted in *Aspects of Irish nationalism* (Belfast, 1972), p. 7.

44 Quoted in Kennedy, *The widening gulf* p. 230.

45 Quoted by John Bowman, 'Inside Ireland', *Sunday Times*, 19 January 1992.

46 J.M. Barkley, *Blackmouth and dissenter* (Belfast, 1991), p. 51.

47 Ulster commentary, N.I.H.S., 27 April 1949 as quoted in Andrew Gailey (ed.) *Crying in the wilderness: Jack Sayers, a liberal editor in Ulster 1939–69* (Belfast, 1995), pp 35–6.

48 Richard Rose, *Governing without consensus: an Irish perspective* (London, 1971), pp 208–17.

49 Brian Faulkner, in *Aquarius*, 1971, p. 89.

50 Quoted in Richard Rose, *Governing without consensus*: (London, 1971), p. 207.

51 Information on first two surveys from Edward Moxon-Browne, 'National identity in Northern Ireland' in Peter Stringer and Gillian Robinson (eds) *Social attitudes in Northern Ireland* (1990–91 edition) (Belfast, 1991), p. 25; the 1993 survey was reported in the *Irish Times*, 19 May 1995.

52 See Fionnuala O'Connor, *In search of a state: catholics in Northern Ireland* (Belfast, 1993).

53 See John A. Murphy, 'Religion and Irish identity' and Dermot Keogh, 'Catholicism and the formation of the modern Irish society' in Princess Grace Irish Library (ed), *Irishness in a changing society* (Gerrards Cross, 1988), pp 132–177.

[54] See Moxon-Browne, 'National identity in Northern Ireland' p. 25, and *Irish Times,* 19 May 1995.

[55] B.B.C. (N.I.), March 1995.

[56] *Irish Times,* 26 August, 28 October and 7 December 1993.

[57] Ibid., 23 October 1995.

[58] Ibid., 17 March 1992.

[59] See D.H. Akenson, *The Irish diaspora – a primer* (Belfast, 1994).

[60] Quoted from typescript of President Robinson's speech, as issued by government information office.

Chapter 7: Historical perspectives in and on Northern Ireland

[1] Foreword by J.C. Beckett to Ciaran Brady, Mary O'Dowd and Brian Walker (eds), *Ulster: an illustrated history* (London, 1989), p. 5. This whole subject is discussed by F.S.L. Lyons in *Culture and anarchy in Ireland, 1880–1939* (Oxford, 1980).

[2] Preface by T.W. Moody and R.D. Edwards, in *Irish Historical Studies,* 1 (1938–9), pp 1–3.

[3] Quoted in J.H. Whyte, *Interpreting Northern Ireland* (Oxford, 1990), p. 122.

[4] Brian Turner, 'The twisting rope – local studies in Ulster' in *Irish Review,* no. 8 (Spring, 1990), pp 47–51.

[5] Ronan Fanning, 'The great enchantment – uses and abuses of modern Irish history' in Ciaran Brady (ed.) *Interpreting Irish history: the debate on historical revisionism* (Dublin, 1994), p. 153.

[6] See *Contents list of historical journals in Northern Ireland,* 1989, published by The Federation of Ulster Local Studies (Belfast, 1989).

[7] Interview by Yvonne Healy in *Irish Times,* 21 July 1995.

Final observations

[1] *Irish Times,* 4 March 1996 and 2 December 1995.

[2] *Belfast Newsletter,* 26 May 1996; *Belfast Telegraph,* 17 September, 1995.

[3] Lord Armstrong, 'Ethnicity, the English and Northern Ireland: comments and reflections' in Dermot Keogh and Michael Haltzel (eds) *Northern Ireland and the politics of reconciliation* (Cambridge, 1993), pp 203–4.

[4] Ronald McNeill, *Ulster's stand for union* (London, 1922), p. 9.

[5] *Report of the international body chaired by Senator George Mitchell, 22 January 1996,* p. 5.

[6] C.C. O'Brien, *Ancestral voices* (Dublin, 1994); J. Bowyer Bell, The Irish troubles: a generation of violence, 1967–92 (Dublin, 1993), p. 829.

7 Vincent Comerford, 'Political myths in modern Ireland' in Princess Grace Irish Library (ed.) *Irishness in a changing society* (Gerrard's Cross, 1988), p. 6.

8 Ibid.

9 *Mitchell Report*, p. 5.

10 F.W. De Klerk, speech to Dublin forum of peace and reconciliation, 21 November, 1995 (typescript), p. 2.

11 Address of R.L. McCartney to 'Vision for the future conference' in Ulster Hall, 27 June 1995 (typescript), p. 2.

12 *Irish Times*, 25, 26 and 27 December 1995 (An Irishman's diary).

INDEX